CHILD WELFARE

JOURNAL OF THE CHILD WELFARE LEAGUE OF AMERICA, INC.
Volume LXII   Number 6   November/December 1983

EDITOR'S PAGE

SPECIAL ISSUE

DEPARTMENTS

To Our Readers

The contents of each issue of CHILD WELFARE normally span the ever-growing range of policies, practices, and programs that characterize today's child welfare field. Readers tell us that that's a good thing because they usually find articles that touch their particular work or interests. Sometimes we find that we can group together two or three articles on one subject. Special issues, however, in which the entire contents are devoted to a single subject, can happen only when the subject is of concern to most readers and suitable manuscript material is available.

The condensed research report this special issue brings to you has several points of particular interest and usefulness. On one hand, what happens after foster care bears directly on the work of most child welfare persons: it is at the heart of permanency planning, and it inevitably constitutes the ultimate test of all forms of substitute child care. On the other hand, it has been little studied. The authors of this research confront both aspects of this paradox by following active cases of children and families, for whom permanency is being planned, into their permanent placements, and by analyzing the outcomes.

Readers should give thought to the nature of the research; many more outcome studies are certain to lie ahead (the League has already published *Recidivism in Foster Care*, by Norman Block and Arlene Libowitz), and validation eventually rests on comparisons of the methodologies and results of cumulative research. The long-sought goal of integration of research and practice, however, can already be seen in this special issue. Agency people on all levels will be especially drawn to the important implications for practice that the authors of this study found. Their recommendations have the ring of practicality. Directions for case management are crystallizing from this and the few studies already published. They deserve the closest attention.

C.S.

After Foster Care: Outcomes of Permanency Planning for Children

EDITH FEIN
ANTHONY N. MALUCCIO
V. JANE HAMILTON
DARRYL E. WARD

Concern has been mounting in the United States over the need to provide permanent families for children who enter foster care. Dissatisfaction with the child welfare system has grown, particularly in regard to its effectiveness in either preventing out-of-home placement* completely, or, if prevention has

---

*The definition of permanency planning is evolving as practitioners and researchers gain more experience with it. Although the most recent definition of permanency planning encompasses the concept of work with families to prevent placement or maintain at home those children who are at risk of placement, this article is concerned only with children who were already out of their homes and for whom planning occurred in order to move them into permanent situations.

Edith Fein, M.A., is Director of Research, Child & Family Services, Hartford, CT. Anthony N. Maluccio, D.S.W., is Professor, The University of Connecticut, School of Social Work, West Hartford, CT. V. Jane Hamilton, Ph.D., was formerly Research Associate, Child & Family Services, Hartford, CT. Darryl E. Ward, M.A. (Social Service Administration), C.A.G.S. (Special Education), is Senior Comprehensive Planner (Human Services) for the county of Morris, Morristown, NJ. Research for this article was funded by Grant Number 90-C-1794 from the Administration for Children, Youth, and Families, U.S. Department of Health & Human Services. The authors deeply appreciate the contributions and cooperation of the clients, staff, and administration of the Connecticut Department of Children and Youth Services.

failed, helping to reunite children with their biological families [Children's Defense Fund 1978].

Development and promotion of plans to ensure permanency or stability for each child have consequently begun to shape the philosophy and goals of many foster care programs. Emphasis on permanent placements has also arisen in an attempt to solve a long-standing service-delivery problem often summarized as "children adrift in foster care." This phrase has been used to describe the instability, uncertainty, and longevity of the child's experience within a placement program that is supposed to be temporary and remedial [Maluccio et al. 1980]. Emphasis on permanency planning also is reflected in the Adoption Assistance and Child Welfare Act of 1980 [Public Law 96-272], which was enacted by the Congress to promote permanent plans for children who come to the attention of the public child welfare system.

Various aspects of the concept of permanency planning are highlighted by different authors. According to Maluccio et al. [1980], permanency planning is a term employed to mean

> philosophical commitment to the vital role of the family in a child's development; continuity of care; adoption; a case management method; systematic case review; a program to reduce the number of children in temporary care. [p. 519]

Emlen et al. [1977:10–11] assert that the quality of permanence includes the following features: (1) the home is not guaranteed to last forever but is "intended to last indefinitely," (2) "permanence means commitment and continuity in the child's relationships," (3) the family is one in which the child has a real sense of belonging and "definite legal status," and (4) the child has "a respected social status" in contrast to the second-class status typical of temporary foster care. Maluccio and Fein [1983a: 197] propose the following definition:

> Permanency planning is the systematic process of carrying out, within a brief, time-limited period, a set of goal-directed activities designed to help children live in families that offer continuity of relationships with nurturing parents or caretakers and the opportunity to establish lifetime relationships.

Although permanency planning thus refers to diverse components and meanings, it essentially embodies a number of key features:

- a philosophy highlighting the value of rearing children in a family setting, preferably their biological families

- a theoretical framework stressing that stability and continuity of relationships promote children's growth and functioning

- a program based on systematic planning within specified time frames for children placed (or at risk of placement) in foster care

- a sense of mutual respect and a spirit of active collaboration among child welfare personnel, lawyers, judges, and others working with children and their parents

- a case management method emphasizing specific practice strategies such as early delineation of long-term plans for the child, legal processes, case reviews, contracting, and decision making, along with active participation of parents in the helping process [Maluccio and Fein 1983a]*

Permanency planning has been substantially promoted through the activities of the landmark Oregon Project, which have included research, demonstration of service delivery, and national dissemination of knowledge through extensive training and technical assistance to child welfare agencies interested in building permanency planning into their programs [Downs et al. 1981, Emlen et al. 1977, Pike et al. 1977, Regional Institute for Human Services 1976.]

---

*For further discussion of the definition and components of permanency planning, see Maluccio and Fein [1983a] and Maluccio and Fein [1983b].

1. Purpose and Context of Study

The tremendous faith that this approach will serve as a panacea for complex problems plaguing foster care has tended to obscure objective examination of permanency planning [Maluccio et al. 1980, Rooney 1982]. In particular, although agencies have been putting efforts into creating plans for stable placements, relatively little attention has been given to what happens to children following discharge. Research has been focused largely on the foster care experience itself.

The study reported here was therefore undertaken to explore the aftercare experiences and functioning of children who left the foster care system to go into placements that were considered stable or permanent. The following questions were addressed:

1. Which children leave foster care and where do they go?

2. Do these children remain in their permanent homes?

3. How well are the children functioning?

4. What services do children and their families need and use, and how are these related to stressful life events?

5. What are the characteristics and needs of the different types of permanent homes?

6. What are the characteristics, histories, and situations of those children whose placements disrupted?

7. How does a caseworker's permanency planning affect outcome?

The study was conducted between 1979 and 1981 and consisted of a longitudinal investigation of a sample of 187 children under the age of 14 who were discharged to a permanent home from temporary foster care, after a stay of at least 30 days, by the Connecticut State Department of Children and Youth Services (DCYS). Unlike investigations of permanency planning that have involved demonstration projects, this study was carried out in the natural context of the regular service delivery of a public child welfare agency. Data were gathered primarily through extensive research interviews with parents or caretakers in the permanent home at three points: up to 4 months after the child moved into the home, 6 to 10 months after placement, and 12 to 16 months after placement. The interviews focused on the parents' or caretakers' perceptions of the children's functioning and adjustment in the family and their needs for, and uses of, formal and informal support systems. Additional data about the children's backgrounds, their placement histories, and the caseworkers' planning were obtained through a review of case records and interviews with agency caseworkers.

The investigation represented the combined efforts of three institutions: Child & Family Services, as the research group; the Connecticut Department of Children and Youth Services, as supplier of the study population; and The University of Connecticut School of Social Work, as the source of graduate students who served as research interviewers. Caseworkers, supervisors, and administrators from the state agency were actively involved in formulating and implementing the study, thus helping to ensure its relevance for practice.

Undertaking research of this nature is especially important at this time, since the historically renewed emphasis on permanency planning will be making increased demands on child welfare agencies, particularly in the public sector. During the next few years, the strengthening of agency efforts in aftercare programs is a likely development to maintain and improve permanent plans for children. Knowledge gathered through studies such as this one could therefore have a major impact on costs and strong implications for changes in practice.

2. Previous Research on Permanency Planning

Because permanency planning is a fundamental, if not always explicit, feature of service delivery, most research in foster care can be viewed as having implications for permanency planning. Research literature especially pertinent to permanency planning includes studies documenting the drift of children in foster care [Fanshel 1971, Jenkins 1967], a longitudinal asssessment of the effects of foster care on children [Fanshel and Shinn 1978], and studies analyzing how different variables are related to duration of foster care [Jenkins 1967, Murphy 1968]. In addition, evaluations of services to parents [Jones, Neuman, and Shyne 1976; Stein, Gambrill, and Wiltse 1978] as well as assessment of case review procedures [Claburn, Magura, and Resnick 1976; Claburn, Magura, and Chizeck 1977; Claburn and Magura 1978] suggest techniques to accomplish permanency planning.

Effectiveness of Services in Preventing Placement

From a narrower viewpoint, there is a growing body of research in which authors specifically identify their studies as dealing with the issues involved in achieving a permanent home. Some of these investigations provide experimental comparisons of regular agency services with intensive services designed to minimize the drift of children in unplanned long-term foster placements. The results are varied.

In one study of 413 children placed through a public child welfare agency, the authors examined the relative effectiveness of the following alternative service approaches: (1) regular services, (2) administrative case monitoring, and (3) administrative case monitoring plus special workers to provide services to parents. They concluded that "it could not be demonstrated to a statistically significant degree that the special intervention strategies worked better than regular practice" [Sherman, Neuman, and Shyne 1973:98]. The authors recognized, however, that the design of their research was not truly experimental, since it was not possible to assign cases randomly to experimental and control groups; the effect of antecedent variables therefore could not be controlled.

These findings differed from another study by Jones, Newman, and Shyne

[1976], who examined a demonstration project involving a sample of 549 families in which it had been determined by a social service agency that there was at least one child at risk of placement in foster care. The purpose of the project, which involved a range of public and private child welfare agencies, was "to test the effectiveness of intensive family casework services to prevent the occurrence or recurrence of foster care placements" [Jones, Newman, and Shyne 1976:118]. Effectiveness was measured by means of outcome criteria such as number of children placed in foster care, duration of placement, whether the child returned to the biological home, and the child's problems and functioning. These researchers concluded that the project was successful in preventing or shortening placement and in helping children and parents. Variables that were positively related to successful outcome included an intensive worker-client relationship and provision of needed services (such as housing and health) to the family.

Studies conducted in public agencies in California and Iowa have demonstrated the effectiveness of using service contracts and case planning to move children out of temporary care more rapidly [Stein, Gambrill, and Wiltse 1978; Iowa Department of Social Services 1977]. Similarly, the Oregon Project found that a higher percentage of project children were in permanent homes than was true for the comparison groups characterized by customary casework activity [Lahti et al. 1978, Lahti and Dvorak 1981]. The project's casework techniques emphasized decision-making guidelines for devising appropriate plans and court procedures for terminating parental rights.

Follow-Up Studies

The findings of the few projects reporting on the outcome of permanent placements in foster care do not provide clear-cut answers on the issue of what happens to the child after a permanent plan is achieved. There are questions, first of all, about the stability of the placements: Are they truly "permanent"? On one hand, the Oregon Project's follow-up study of 259 children revealed that 90% of the children remained in the same placement 18 months later, with adoptive homes being the most stable and having the fewest disruptions, although this difference was not statistically significant [Lahti et al. 1978]. On the other hand, another study found that only 66% (19 out of 29) of children discharged from a time-limited foster care program remained in their permanent placements at the point of follow-up (19 to 24 months); however, this program served primarily emotionally disturbed children, which may account for the discrepancy [Fein, Davies, and Knight 1979]. These researchers found no difference in stability of placement between discharges to adoptive and biological parents.

The results of a broader investigation at the New Jersey State Division of Youth and Family Services suggested evidence that the findings of the Fein, Davies, and Knight [1979] study of emotionally disturbed youngsters may also be true of other populations [Claburn, Magura, and Chizeck 1977]. In the New Jersey study, a follow-up of a sample of 612 children who had spent at least one week in out-of-home placements showed that 19% of those discharged had at least one distinct reopening of their cases during a 4½-year period. This figure, moreover, does not include additional children who may have re-entered the foster care system in other ways, for example, through out-of-state and private agency placements.

In a comprehensive study conducted in New York City, it was found that, by the end of 5 years, 16% of the 381 children in the sample had been returned to foster care at least once [Fanshel and Shinn 1978:159]. Again, however, these figures do not account for additional children who may have experienced other types of changes in their discharge placements. In another study at a New York private agency, 28% of the 314 children discharged from foster care in 1978 and 1979 were returned to care [Block 1981:601]. The study population consisted of children under the age of 18 who had been returned to their biological parents or placed with relatives, friends, or new adoptive parents.

Looking beyond the sole aspect of permanence, several studies have also examined whether there were any differences in adjustment between those children in permanent homes and those remaining in temporary foster care. Two investigations found no difference between these types of placement [Iowa Department of Social Services 1977; Jones, Newman, and Shyne 1976], a finding that is consistent with the longitudinal evaluation of the effects of foster care carried out by Fanshel and Shinn [1978].

In the follow-up study of the Oregon Project it was found that there was no difference in adjustment between the children in temporary foster care and those in permanent placements. These investigators noted, moreover, that the child's and the parents' or caretakers' sense of permanence, rather than the legal status of the placement, seemed to be most closely related to the child's well-being [Lahti et al. 1978:9.3].

Earlier studies that specifically addressed the after-foster-care issue looked at their subjects in adult life, rather than concentrating on the events immediately subsequent to the foster care experience, and relied on small samples [Gil 1964, Meier 1965]. More important, the results of these studies refer to foster care situations of many years ago and have few implications for today's practice. The authors reported on a service structure in which it was not uncommon for over half of the recipients to spend more than 7 years in foster care [Maas and Engler 1959].

Similarly, there has been a dearth of research on barriers that deter permanency planning. A major contribution was the Oregon Project's analysis of barriers, but this study was conducted in the context of a demonstration project [Emlen et al. 1977, Regional Research Institute for Human Services 1976].

The studies reviewed here, for the most part, are limited in applicability: they did not differentiate children in foster care by variables such as aftercare and placement history and did not supply information that could help determine how permanency planning needs differ among different types of children. In addition, most of the data gathered were from demonstration projects or special intensive services, which suggests the possibility of a Hawthorne effect in the findings: the studies did not investigate how permanency planning operates in the more typical context of a large public social service system, which has the greatest potential for applicability to present child welfare practice.

3. Design and Methodology

As previously noted, the purpose of this research was to explore the aftercare experiences and functioning of children placed in permanent homes from foster care and the effects of permanency planning on the maintenance of the placements. The study was a follow-up investigation of 187 children, ages 0–14 years, who had been in foster care for at least 30 days and were placed in one of the following types of permanent homes: (1) biological homes, (2) adoptive homes, (3) homes with relatives, (4) permanent foster homes, or (5) foster parent adoptive homes (this was a status change occurring at the time the decision to adopt was made). Data were collected from the case records, from brief interviews with the caseworkers assigned to each case, and from extensive interviews with the parents or caretakers at the permanent homes.

Setting of the Study

The study was conducted by the Research Department of Child & Family Services, with the cooperation of the Department of Children and Youth Services (DCYS) of the State of Connecticut. DCYS is a comprehensive state-wide children's services agency with statutory responsibility for all child welfare, child mental health, and juvenile delinquency services. At the time the study began, Connecticut was one of several states that had such a single-purpose agency serving children. The DCYS Division of Children's and Protective Services, which included its foster care program, had a stated policy of treatment planning and permanency planning for all youngsters in its care.

Procedure for Obtaining Consent

Many planning meetings with the central office staff and the regional office staffs of DCYS were held to set up a procedure for obtaining signed informed consents from potential subjects. There was concern that the rights of parents and children be protected. The procedure that proved most comfortable legally, ethically, and professionally for the research staff and for DCYS required the child's DCYS caseworker to obtain the signed consent from the parent or caretaker at the time the youngster was placed in the permanent home or as

494

soon thereafter as possible. If necessary, as an alternative, the caseworker explained the study on the telephone to the parent or caretaker, obtained a verbal consent, and had the research interviewer get a signed consent after further explanation in person. These two alternatives, which were used for the entire study sample, occasionally resulted in lapses of time that aged cases beyond a period acceptable for interviewing.*

Interview Instruments and Procedures

Caretaker Interviews

None of the studies that had been done on children leaving foster care were appropriate for this population, considering the purposes of the study. Accordingly, new interview instruments were developed, seeking information about:

1. family characteristics;

2. the child's functioning in school;

3. the child's overall emotional adjustment and behavior;

4. the family's use of support systems;

5. the family's need for, and use of, services;

6. the child's attitudes;

7. the caretaker's attitudes about the child's placement.

Most questions in the hour-long interview applied to all respondents, but some were limited to certain placement types or to placements of older children. The "child behavior" section was prepared in four forms for use with children of different ages: up to 2.5 years, 2.5 to 6 years, 6 to 12 years, and 12 years and older.

The interviews were scheduled for three different time periods: Interview I: up to 4 months after the date of the child's placement in a permanent home; Interview II: 6 to 10 months after the date of placement; Interview III: 12 to 16 months after the date of placement. The time between interviews in each case was at least 3 months and no more than 6 months.

---

*Copies of the consent form and all other instruments used in the study can be obtained from Edith Fein, Director of Research, Child & Family Services, 1680 Albany Avenue, Hartford, CT 06105.

Each of the interview forms was translated into Spanish. The forms were pre-tested on 7 families with children who previously had been in the Child & Family Services foster care program. Minor modifications were made according to the findings.

Interviewers

Most interviewers were students at the University of Connecticut School of Social Work, some were DCYS caseworkers who interviewed only outside the region in which they worked, and a few were social workers employed in private agencies. All were trained by the research staff before each interview phase. A training manual was also prepared on how to set up and conduct the research interview.

Interview Procedures

After a child was identified and caretaker consent to be interviewed was obtained through the caseworker, the child's case was assigned to an interviewer. The race of the child's caretaker and interviewer were matched whenever possible. For 70% of the study population, the interviewers were the same race as the caretakers.

The assigned interviewer telephoned, or made a home visit if the caretaker did not have a phone, to set up a mutually convenient appointment. At least three attempts or visits were made to locate caretakers before they were considered impossible to contact.

Assurance was given to respondents that the study was independent from DCYS, that non-participation would not affect any services they received from state agencies, and that all information disclosed would remain confidential. Many respondents said that they valued the interview as a way to bring out their accomplishments, frustrations, and concerns.

Case Record Information and Caseworker Interviews

An additional source of data on the children in the study was their case records, on file at the DCYS regional offices. Information extracted from the records included demographic data; reasons for case opening or foster care placement, since they were sometimes different; foster care history; legal aspects of the child's case; and the date that the current DCYS worker was assigned the case.

In addition to obtaining data from the records, an interview was completed with each child's caseworker, either in person or by telephone. The caseworkers were asked about the permanent plan that had been chosen for each child, the barriers to accomplishing the placement plan, and other plans they may have considered.

Implementation of the Study: Collaboration with DCYS

A substantial amount of time was spent building relationships with DCYS, the source of the study sample. Research staff members met on separate occasions with central administrators, the 5 regional directors in the state and their 11 program supervisors, and the case supervisors and caseworkers in each office. After the study began, periodic progress reports were written and verbal reports were presented to regional directors and program supervisors at their regular meetings and to the Central Office staff member appointed as liaison to the research study.

This extensive reporting was planned into the study because of the contributions by caseworkers to the design of the study, the interest shown by many during the case identification and data collection phases, and high caseworker turnover in state agencies. It was felt that such presentations would help maintain interest over the entire course of the study.

Among the reports presented to them, caseworkers were especially interested in the descriptions of the children from their offices compared to the state as a whole, since at the time of the study they did not have descriptive information on the children in foster care or those leaving the system. Information about sex, age, type of permanent home, and number of foster care placements gave caseworkers a general idea of trends in the exit of children from foster care. Caseworkers were also concerned about the aftercare experiences of the children and their families, especially the services and supports that helped maintain the placement. The existing rapport between research staff members and the DCYS workers was strengthened through these meetings. Sustaining this unique relationship was an important accomplishment.

Pre-Study Activities

In the year before the intake period of the study, several meetings were held with members of the DCYS central administration, who indicated that the research questions were timely and consistent with their concerns. DCYS administration staff members also helped to formulate additional research questions and gave their approval to the department's participation in the study.

Study Activities

To facilitate state-wide cooperation, obtain information from regional offices about their procedures, and inform staff members about research concerns, introductory meetings were arranged with each of the 11 area offices during May and June 1979. These meetings were designed to give all workers information about the research study, answer their questions, respond to their objections, and obtain their participation.

Many questions and issues were raised in all meetings, especially on the specifics of data gathering, the issue of confidentiality of clients' responses, and the roles of the workers in the study. The wording of the consent forms was thoroughly discussed and changes were made on the basis of the comments and suggestions received in the meetings. A great deal of information about the practices in each office was gained in the meetings. Many minor, and some major, differences in procedures among offices were found, which helped the research staff to plan the specific methods of case identification and develop the interview instruments.

Procedures for Identification of Cases

A major problem in implementing the study was identifying children who had left foster care. No such listing existed. Dates of case closings were more readily obtainable but did not usually coincide with the dates of exit from foster care. Since the study was designed to obtain information at the point of discharge, when the new adjustments required of child and family may be greatest, the timely identification of cases was critical. Many attempts were made to create systems that would identify the children who left foster care.

After testing various approaches, it became necessary to resort to a cumbersome and time-consuming plan. Caseworkers in each office were telephoned by research staff members every week or two to identify children on their individual caseloads who were moving out of foster care. A total of 308 caseworkers were called periodically by project staff members to obtain the study population. This heroic effort proved successful, although many cases were lost because of time delays; the original 6-month study intake period, therefore, had to be extended by 2½ months to obtain a reasonable sample size.

Analysis of Data

Analysis of data ranged from simple descriptive presentations to more complex inferential tests. The major experimental questions involved determination of the relative contributions of the independent variables (e.g., children's age, sex, number of placements) and intervening variables (e.g., type of permanent home, caseworker's planning) to the outcomes measured by the dependent variables (e.g., Family Adjustment). Multiple regression analysis was used to examine the degree of relationship of several independent variables to each of the dependent variables. This regression procedure was carried out on data obtained at each of the three interview periods and on data obtained from the differences between Interviews I and III. The analysis of data was strengthened by the repeated assessments of subjects over time, permitting the determination of changes over time and of the most valuable predictors among the independent variables.

As data were summarized, it was found that the study children who were up to 2½ years of age differed in many respects from the children in other age groups. First, their scores on the outcome measures were significantly higher than the other groups ($t < .05$). In fact, there was a distinct ceiling effect, with some of the children receiving the highest possible score. Also, a number of interview items in the outcome scores were not appropriate to this age group (e.g., How long do you think this child expects to stay here?). This group of 49 very young children was therefore treated separately; descriptive information regarding them is presented but they are not included in the main statistical analyses.

4. Study Sample

Representativeness of the Study Sample

Of the 726 children identified by DCYS as moving into permanent placements between July 1, 1979, and March 15, 1980, most (73%) were returned to their biological parents. The other children were placed either in adoptive homes (13%), with relatives (6%), in permanent foster homes (6%), or were adopted by their foster parents (3%). Compared to the entire group leaving foster care, in the research study sample of 187 children, those returned to their biological parents were somewhat underrepresented (53%); those in adoptive homes were overrepresented (24%). Percentages of the children in the sample in other placement types were roughly similar to the larger group (see table 1).

Most children moved into a permanent placement after being in foster family care, although 17% came from residential care. The 2½- to 14-year-olds had been in care an average of 24.8 months, with 2.3 previous placements.

As seen in table 2, of the entire group leaving foster care, more boys (62%) than girls (38%) were placed in permanent homes. The research study sample included percentages of boys and girls (64% and 36%) similar to the entire group.

It can also be seen in table 2 that the age distribution in the study sample was almost identical to that of the entire group of children leaving foster care. Additionally, more infants and toddlers (under 3 years old) moved into permanent homes than children from any other age group, and the number of children in each of the other age groups (3 to 5, 6 to 8, 9 to 11, 12 and over) was similar.

Racially, whites were somewhat overrepresented and other races underrepresented in the study sample. These percentages differed according to regional office, with those in the larger urban areas having higher concentrations of specific racial groups.

Reasons for Loss of Cases

The study sample at Interview I represents 26% of the entire group of children leaving foster care who fit the study criteria and moved into a permanent home between July 1, 1979, and March 15, 1980. The reasons for so many children

TABLE 1 Children in Each Type of Permanent Home

Type of Permanent Home	All DCYS Children Who Fit Study Criteria and Moved Into Permanent Homes During Intake Phase of the Study		Children in Study Sample	
	(N)	(%)	(N)	(%)
Biological	529	73	100	53
Adoptive	93	13	45	24
Permanent Foster	42	6	14	7
Relatives'	40	6	15	8
Foster Parent Adoptive	22	3	13	7
Total	726	101	187	99

Percentages may not add up to 100% because figures were rounded.

TABLE 2 Sex, Age, and Race of Children in the Study Sample and Population

	DCYS Population* (N = 726)		Study Sample (N = 187)	
	(N)	(%)	(N)	(%)
Sex				
Male	450	62	120	64
Female	276	38	67	36
Age				
Under 3 years	214	29	56	30
3 to 5 years	129	18	30	16
6 to 8 years	124	17	28	15
9 to 11 years	139	19	42	22
12 years and older	115	16	31	16
Missing	5			
Race				
White	458	63	140	75
Black	159	22	32	17
Hispanic	66	9	7	4
Mixed	32	4	8	4
Missing	11	2	—	—

Percentages may not add up to 100% because figures were rounded.

* All DCYS children who fit study criteria and moved into permanent homes during the intake phase of the study.

not becoming a part of the study sample were examined to determine if particular reasons were related to one type of permanent home or one age group of children. Such systematic bias did not appear, since similar reasons occurred in all types of permanent homes and age groups.

Refusal of caretakers to be interviewed accounted for only 11% of the loss of children's cases from the research sample. The largest loss was caused by reasons involving caseworkers, and it affected all placement types. Caseworkers' refusal to attempt to obtain consent and caseworkers' delays in case identification and obtaining consent accounted for 33% of the loss. The reasons given by the caseworkers for refusing to attempt to obtain consent were lack of time, negative feelings about research, and "protectiveness" or concern for the client's confidentiality. Other reasons for loss of children's cases included inability to locate a caretaker or set up an interview within the allotted time period (17%), disruption of the placement before the first interview (5%), interview completed after time limit (3%), placement of more than two siblings (2%), and missing reason (2%).

By Interview II, the most frequent reason for the lost cases (34) was the inability to reach or locate the caretaker for an interview (22 cases). Only four caretakers refused to participate in the second interview.

At Interview III, 31 cases were lost from the sample. Again, the most common reason was inability to reach or locate the caretaker (22 cases), followed by cases in which the caretaker was unwilling to be interviewed because the child was no longer in the home (4 cases).

Interview I Sample

There were 187 children in the study sample and all were included at Interview I. Of these children, 100 (53%) had been returned to their biological homes, 45 (24%) had been placed in adoptive homes, 14 (7%) had been placed in permanent foster homes, 15 (8%) had been placed in relatives' homes, and 13 (7%) were being adopted by their foster parents.

As shown in table 3, 120 of the 187 children were male (64%) and the remaining 67 (36%) were female. The proportions of males and females in each type of permanent placement were not significantly different.

The ages of the children are displayed also in table 3, where it can be seen that most of the adopted children were under the age of 3 and most of the children adopted by foster parents were under the age of 6.

Table 4 shows the racial composition of the 187 children in the sample. Significantly more white children (36%) than black children (13%) went to adoptive or foster parent adoptive homes, and a greater percentage of black

TABLE 3 Sex and Age of Children in Each Type of Permanent Home
(N = 187)

Type of Permanent Home

	Biological		Adoptive		Permanent Foster		Relatives		Foster Parent Adoptive		Total	
	(N)	(%)	(N)	(%)	(N)	(%)	(N)	(%)	(N)	(%)	(N)	(%)
Sex												
Male	68	68	27	60	11	78	7	47	7	54	120	64
Female	32	32	18	40	3	21	8	53	6	46	67	36
Age												
Under 3 years	21	21	28	62	—	—	2	13	5	38	56	30
3 to 5 years	19	19	5	11	2	14	1	7	3	23	30	16
6 to 8 years	17	17	7	16	3	21	1	7	—	—	28	15
9 to 11 years	30	30	3	7	3	21	4	27	2	15	42	22
12 years and older	13	13	2	4	6	43	7	47	3	23	31	17

Percentages may not add up to 100% because figures were rounded.

TABLE 4   Race of Children in Each Type of Permanent Home

Type of Permanent Home	White		Black		Hispanic		Mixed		Total
	(N)	(%)	(N)	(%)	(N)	(%)	(N)	(%)	(N)
Biological	68	48	21	66	6	86	5	62	100
Adoptive	41	29	3	9	—	—	1	12	45
Permanent Foster	13	9	1	3	—	—	—	—	14
Relatives'	8	6	6	19	—	—	1	12	15
Foster Parent Adoptive	10	7	1	3	1	14	1	12	13
Total	140	99	32	100	7	100	8	98	187

Percentages may not add to 100% because of rounding.

children than white were returned to their biological or relatives' homes. Of the 7 Hispanic children, 6 were returned to their biological homes and the seventh was being adopted by the foster parents. Although children with mixed racial backgrounds were placed in several situations, most were returned to their biological homes.

There were 29 sets of siblings (58 children) who were placed together. Twenty-one sets had been returned to their biological homes, 4 sets were adopted, 2 sets were being adopted by their foster parents, 1 set was placed with relatives, and 1 set was placed with permanent foster parents.

Interview II Sample

Of the 187 children in the original study sample, 153 (82%) were available at Interview II. There were no significant differences in the proportions of children in each type of permanent home.

The male-to-female ratio at Interview II also was not significantly different from the original group; 66% were male, 34% were female. In addition, the proportion of males and females in each type of permanent home was not significantly different from the proportions at Interview I.

In regard to the ages of children at Interview II, the sample proportion in each age group was similar to those at Interview I.

The number of siblings placed together, however, decreased among those who had been returned to their biological homes, from 21 sets at Interview I to 14 sets by Interview II, but the decrease was not statistically significant.

Interview III Sample

Of the 187 children in the original study sample, 122 (65%) remained at Interview III. The trends in the sample loss at Interview III remained generally the same as those between Interviews I and II.

The male-to-female ratio at all three interviews remained stable, approximately 62% male to 38% female. The sex ratio of the children placed with relatives changed, however. At Interview I there were 7 males and 8 females; at Interview III this changed to 1 male and 7 females.

In regard to age and race, there were no significant differences in the distribution of the Interview III sample compared with Interview I.

5. Children's Functioning

Analysis Plan

The data on the 138 2½- to 14-year-old children* were analyzed to determine which characteristics of the children and their placement histories and permanent homes were related to the children's functioning, as well as the extent to which these factors were interrelated. The information in the literature about children leaving foster care is limited, and no major model describing their adjustment explains or predicts outcomes. When the goal is to examine the relationship between several independent variables (e.g., child's age, sex, race) and one dependent variable or outcome (e.g., family adjustment), multiple regression analysis can be employed to demonstrate the contributions of each of the independent variables in explaining the outcome. Regression analyses were used to answer these questions:

1. How much of the variation in the outcome scores (children's functioning) can be accounted for by selected independent variables?

2. Which variables add significantly to the change in outcome?

The dependent variables were the four outcome measures: the child's Family Adjustment, Emotional and Developmental Functioning, Child Behavior, and School Functioning. Selected characteristics of the child and the permanent home were the independent regressor variables. The analysis was done at each of the three interview times and also for changes over time, that is, using the Interview III minus Interview I difference scores.

Some of the variables in this analysis were continuous or scaled (e.g., age) but others were categorical (e.g., sex, race) and therefore transformed into dichotomies that could be analyzed in a regression procedure. Some of the variables remained the same in each time period (e.g., sex, race, type of permanent home) while others were time-specific (e.g., marital status, number of children in the home.) Time-specific variables were updated at each interview time.

Because only school-age children had outcome scores in school functioning, there was a large reduction in the number of children in the school functioning analysis. In order to sustain statistical power it therefore was

---

* Among the 187 children in the study sample, there were 49 children aged 2½ years or younger. Data for these children are analyzed separately in section 7 (Infants and Toddlers).

necessary to reduce the number of independent variables that were entered in the regression analysis. This was accomplished by removing three of the variables concerning permanent home characteristics (marital status, income, and number of children) that were believed to be less directly related to school functioning than the other variables.

In addition, the data were analyzed to determine which planning variables were related to outcome. Again, the four outcome measures (Family Adjustment, Emotional and Developmental Functioning, Child Behavior, and School Functioning) were dependent variables, and selected planning and casework aspects (e.g., barriers to placement, pre-placement services used) obtained from casework interviews were independent variables. A stepwise multiple regression analysis was employed to answer the following questions:

1. How much variation in the outcome scores can be explained by the 14 independent planning and casework variables taken in combination?

2. Which of the independent variables add significantly to the amount of variation that is explained?

In addition to the analysis of data at each of the three interview times, an analysis was planned of changes over time. Difference scores were used because of the consistency of the variances of outcome over time periods and because of the assumptions underlying that analysis, namely, that some independent variables such as age, sex, and type of permanent home would affect outcome over time rather than only at the initial interview and that differences between groups might be maintained over the course of the study [Judd and Kenny 1981]. Therefore, difference scores were computed and used for a fourth analysis: Interview III minus Interview I.

Independent Variables

The independent variables fell into two main groups, both logically and on the basis of the source from which they were obtained. The first group consisted of child characteristics, permanent home characteristics, and the child's placement history. Detailed information was available on the child's past foster placements since it was DCYS policy for caseworkers to file a form each time the child was moved. The permanent home characteristics were obtained during interviews with the parent or caretaker at the permanent home, and were updated at each interview time. The variables were:

• Type of permanent home

• Age of child

• Sex of child

- Race of child

- Child's previous placement home

- Number of temporary foster placements since the most recent opening of the case

- Number of times returned to biological home in the past

- Marital status of present parent or caretaker

- Number of children in permanent home

- Income of family

The second group of independent variables consisted of planning and casework data and included information on casework planning for the move to a permanent home, barriers to the accomplishment of the plan, caseworker and parental contact with the child before the move to the permanent home, and caseworker contact after the move. This information came primarily from casework interviews that, because of time constraints, were not as detailed as those with the caretakers in the permanent homes. The data were frequently in the form of yes-or-no responses, particularly with respect to pre-placement activities and barriers to the placement. Occasionally, the caseworker who planned the move had left the agency and the interview was held with the worker who currently had the case but did not have detailed knowledge of the planning activities.

Family Adjustment

The majority of children showed a relatively good family adjustment based on their Family Adjustment scores, although there was a wide range of scores. Using a scale of 1 to 4 (1.00 = poor to 4.00 = very good), the mean score for 134 children for whom scores were available at Interview I was 3.35. The mean for 108 children at Interview II was 3.33; at Interview III it was 3.40 for 79 children.

Interview I

At Interview I, 37% of the variance in Family Adjustment scores accounted for by a number of independent variables statistically significant at the .05 level were: age of the child (older children scored lower than younger children), type of permanent home (children who had been placed with relatives or children who were adopted by their foster parents did better than all other children), race (black children scored highest), previous return home from foster care (children who had been returned home in the past did better than those who had not), previous placement (children who had been in foster placement with relatives immediately prior to the permanent home scored higher than those in non-relative placements), and income (children placed in families with incomes below $10,000 had lower adjustment scores than those in families with incomes above $10,000).

Interview II

At Interview II, 46% of the variance in Family Adjustment outcome was explained by the following statistically significant independent variables: age (older children scored lower), marital status (children with single parents with no other adult in the home scored lowest), previous return home (children who had previously been returned home from foster care scored higher), type of permanent home (children in foster parent adoptive homes scored highest), number of children in the home (children in homes with larger numbers of children scored higher), type of previous placement (children who had previously been in foster homes with relatives scored highest), and race (black children scored highest).

Interview III

At Interview III, 34% of the variance in Family Adjustment scores was explained by the variables in the regression analysis. The statistically significant variables were: age (older children scored lower), previous return home (children previously returned home scored higher), type of permanent home (children in foster parent adoptive and permanent foster homes scored highest), race (black children scored highest), income (children in low-income homes scored lower), marital status (children in homes of single parents with no other adults in the home scored lowest).

Interview III Minus Interview I

The difference scores on the Family Adjustment measure were not significant. The mean difference in scores was only − .07.

Emotional and Developmental Functioning

On a scale of 1 to 4 (1.00 = poor to 4.00 = very good), the mean score on the child's Emotional and Developmental Functioning measure for the 134

2½- to 14-year-old children for whom scores were available at Interview I was 2.85. The mean for Interview II was 2.90 (108 children); for Interview III it was 2.97 (82 children for whom scores were available).

Interview I

At Interview I, 26% of the variance was accounted for in the analysis by five statistically significant variables: number of previous returns to biological homes (children who had been returned home in the past scored higher), number of previous temporary foster placements (children with more placements scored lowest), race (Hispanic children scored highest), type of permanent home (children in relatives' homes scored highest), and age at permanent placement (older children scored lower than younger children).

Interview II

At Interview II, 37% of the variance was accounted for in the analysis by eight statistically significant variables: number of children in the home (children in homes with larger numbers of children scored higher), number of previous returns home (children previously returned home scored higher), age of children (older children scored lower), number of previous temporary foster placements (children with more temporary placements scored lower), type of previous placement (children who had previously been in foster homes with relatives scored highest), marital status (children with single parents with no other adults in the home scored lowest), type of permanent home (children in permanent foster homes scored lowest), and race (Hispanic children scored highest). Four of these variables—age of child, race, number of previous temporary placements, and number of previous returns home—were also significant at Interview I but with one difference: children in placement with relatives scored significantly higher than other children at Interview I but not at Interview II.

Interview III

At Interview III, none of the variables, singly or in combination, were predictive of outcomes.

Interview III Minus Interview I

None of the variables, singly or in combination, were predictive of outcomes.

Child Behavior

On a scale of 0 to 1 (0 = poor, 1.00 = very good), the mean score of 124 children for whom ratings were available at Interview I was 0.72; at Interview II, 0.73 (108 children); and at Interview III, 0.74 (81 children for whom scores were available).

Interview I

None of the variables, singly or in combination, were predictive of outcomes.

Interview II

At Interview II, a number of variables were found to be statistically significant in the analysis: type of permanent home (children in foster parent adoptive homes and children in relatives' homes scored highest), the number of children in the home (children in homes with more children scored higher), race (black children scored lowest), and previous placement (children whose previous placement had been in residential care scored lowest).

Interview III

None of the variables, singly or in combination, were predictive of outcomes.

Interview III Minus Interview I

None of the variables, singly or in combination, were predictive of outcomes.

School Functioning

The examination of the child's School Functioning was not included with the other outcomes because the analysis employed a restricted number of independent variables due to the smaller number of children who had School Functioning scores. The mean score on the School Functioning measure (based on 10 interview items) for the 82 children in the first interview was 3.24 on a scale of 1 to 4 (1.00 = poor to 4.00 = very good). At the second interview, it was 3.25 for the 50 children in the analysis; the third interview mean was 3.42 for 58 children. The second interview sample was smaller than the third because 20 of 71 second interviews involved children on summer vacations whose school outcome scores could not be computed.

Interview I

At Interview I, the overall regression analysis was statistically significant at the .05 level, with 28% of the variance explained by five variables: the sex of the child (females scored higher), the previous placement home (children previously in a foster placement with relatives scored highest), the number of temporary placements (children with more previous placements scored lower), the type of permanent home (children in adoptive homes scored highest), the number of previous returns to the biological home (children returned home in the past scored higher).

Interview II

At Interview II, none of the variables, singly or in combination, were predictive of outcomes. This was the time, however, when many children were on summer vacation; numbers were therefore small.

Interview III

At Interview III, none of the variables, singly or in combination, were predictive of outcomes at the .05 level.

Interview III Minus Interview I

The *F* value in this analysis did not reach significance at the .05 level.

Relationship of Selected Planning and Casework Variables to Outcomes

One of the goals of the study had been to determine whether those children for whom permanency planning had occurred would have better outcomes than those children for whom there was no permanency planning. This goal could not be achieved because all caseworkers stated that they had been planning for a permanent home for the child. An examination was therefore made of other data that had been gathered on the extent of the planning. This information had been collected as a supplement to the planning/no planning dichotomy. It consisted of the types of pre-placement activities that had occurred, along with the caseworkers' perceptions of barriers to their plans.

Although the information used in the regression analyses previously discussed came from case records and caretaker interviews, the planning variables (with the exception of caseworker contact after permanent placement) were collected from brief caseworker interviews, a source of data

6 Reasons
to Enter
Your Own Personal Subscription to CHILD WELFARE

1. You won't have to wait until the routing slip reaches your desk. You'll have authoritative articles on child welfare policy, practice and program as soon as they appear—at home or at work—wherever you choose.

2. You'll receive a wealth of practical ideas and strategies to help you do a better job. And they'll be yours to keep.

3. You'll have access to CHILD WELFARE material for as long as you like . . . a ready reference of workable answers to persistent problems.

4. CHILD WELFARE's unique position as the sole provider of useful information to the child welfare field means it is devoted to your needs and goals; you deserve to give it all the time and attention you want.

5. A chance to read and digest indepth articles, issues extended to accommodate articles of extraordinary length, special issues devoted to a single subject; regular features such as Note Bene, Folio, Reader's Forum; full-length Book Reviews and concise Book Briefs; Information, Please!

6. The only journal offering you "book club" privileges through a Special Publications Subscription . . . bringing you every book published by the Child Welfare League during the calendar year, plus a full year's subscription to CHILD WELFARE. A full resource library at your fingertips.

ORDER FORM   Dept. 8020

Please enter my subscription to CHILD WELFARE (6 issues per year) under the plan indicated below: ☐ This is a renewal.

PLAN 1: Regular Subscription

	1-YR	2-YR
☐ **Individual**	$16	$30

Applicable only to subscriptions paid by personal check.

| ☐ **Institution** | $25 | $45 |

Includes libraries, agencies, government offices, schools, and organizations.

| ☐ **Student** | $12 | |

(Add Canadian and foreign postage—$3.00 per year.)

PLAN 2: Special Publications Subscription

Includes a regular subscription to the journal, and all CWLA books and monographs published during the calendar year.

	1-YR	2-YR
☐ **Individual**	$ 72	$135
☐ **Institution**	$108	$195

☐ Payment enclosed

☐ Bill my ( ) Master Charge ( ) Visa

_____
credit card number

_____
card expiration date

Signature: _____

_____
Name

_____
School/Institution (if applicable)

_____
Address

_____
City   State   Zip

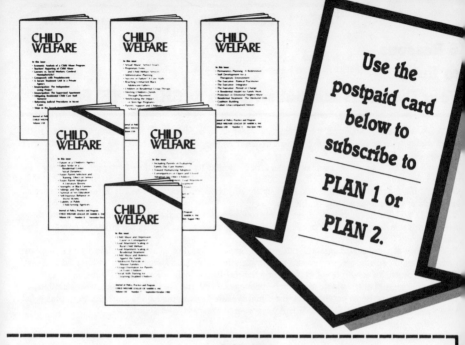

Use the postpaid card below to subscribe to

PLAN 1 or

PLAN 2.

having more drawbacks than any other used in the study. Most of the caseworkers could give only a short period of time to the interviewers and there were, therefore, limitations on the amount of detail that could be obtained. In several cases, the caseworkers who had done most of the planning had left the agency and the data were based on information obtained from their replacements. Nine cases had to be eliminated from the analysis because the plan toward which they had been working was not accomplished.

The information, moreover, was primarily in the form of yes-or-no responses, a restricted range of answers that is less than ideal in discriminating differences between cases. The number of independent variables was also large relative to the number of cases in the analysis, but a sound theoretical basis for further reductions in the number of variables could not be found.

Multiple regression analysis of planning and casework variables with the four dependent variables (the child's scores on Family Adjustment, Emotional and Developmental Functioning, Child Behavior, and School Fuctioning) at Interviews I, II, III, and III minus I was employed. In view of the limitations of the data, it is not surprising that only two of the outcome analyses revealed significant findings: correlations between planning variables and some aspect of Child Behavior and School Functioning at Interview II. Because of the large number of regressions and the fact that no other analysis of Child Behavior revealed significant relationships, this finding should be viewed with caution.

Summary

At each of the three interview times but not for the difference score analysis, the following variables were significantly related to the child's Family Adjustment scores: age of the child, race of the child, the number of previous returns to the biological home, and the type of permanent home. Three of these variables (age of the child, race of the child, and the number of previous returns home) were also significantly related to the Emotional and Developmental Functioning of the children at Interviews I and II. Other variables that were significant for both of these outcomes at least at one interview time were the number of previous foster placements, the previous placement home, marital status, income, and the number of children in the home. The analysis of the Child Behavior outcomes was significant at only one interview time. Because the measure was not standardized and the intercorrelation is low, this analysis should be viewed with caution.

The child's age and placement history variables seem to have a major impact on outcome. Children with more previous placements had lower outcome scores than those with fewer placements. Children who had been previously placed in their biological homes from foster care (even if they were not in biological homes at the time of the study) had better outcomes. Children who had been in foster placements with relatives immediately before the permanent placement were also adjusting better than those who had been in non-relative foster homes or residential care.

The race of the child was also a factor in both the Family Adjustment and Emotional and Developmental Functioning outcomes. Black children were doing better than white children on the Family Adjustment measure at all interview times; Hispanic children were doing best at some interview times.

The only variables in the child's School Functioning that were statistically significant at the .05 level were at Interview I. Certain variables at Interview III approached that level. The sex of the child appeared to be a major factor in accounting for the variations in school outcomes, as did variables relating to placement history in foster care at Interview I.

Some of the characteristics of the permanent home also contributed to the explanation of variance in outcomes. Children in placements with relatives or in foster parent adoptive homes had the highest adjustment scores. Children with single parents (never married, divorced, separated, or widowed) and with no other adult in the home were adjusting poorest. Children in families with incomes of less than $10,000 a year were also lower in Family Adjustment (but not in Emotional Adjustment) than children in families with higher incomes. Another significant variable in the analysis was the number of children in the home; children in homes with a larger number of children had better outcomes.

Although the particular planning variables included in this analysis did not demonstrate significant effects on outcomes, it cannot be assumed that planning itself does not relate to outcome. Further study with more detailed information on the course of planning, the involvement of each party and outside agencies, alternative plans considered, extent and effect of barriers, the difficulties presented by the children (including professional evaluations of emotional problems), and the child's past history of placements would be important in learning more about the relationship between planning and outcome.

6. Services and Supports

One of the goals of the study was to understand better the families' need for, and use of, community services and supports. General questions about services such as housing, counseling, and recreational services were asked of the parents or caretakers at all three interviews. Information was also gathered concerning the barriers impeding or preventing service delivery.

The most comprehensive picture of service use came from information gathered over the longest time period; therefore, the data in this section are from the 107 families of the children who had completed all three interviews. Although there were 122 children in the study at this point, there were only 107 individual caretakers or families because 15 families had 2 children returned to them. The information encompasses an approximate 12- to 16-month time span after placement in the permanent home.

Service Need and Use

According to the caretakers interviewed, the services that were needed the most by families of more than half of the children were medical and dental services, recreational services, counseling, special education or training, and legal services (table 5). A sizable number also felt the need for income assistance, day care, employment counseling, and housing.

Medical and dental services were in the highest demand and also were the most used. Nearly all of the families used these services during the study period.

Recreational services were needed by the families of 82 (67%) of the children and had been used at some point by 63 (77%) of those needing them. Many caretakers said that their families could not take advantage of recreational opportunities available in the community because of lack of funds or transportation.

Counseling services, such as family counseling and referrals to mental health clinics, psychologists, or psychiatrists, were also in high demand: 79 of the families of the 122 children (65%) needed them. Sixty-two (78%) of those needing counseling services reported that they had used them.

There was also a need expressed for special education or training for some

TABLE 5   Need for and Use of Community Services as Reported by Caretakers at Interview III

Service[a]	Need for Service[b] (N = 122)		Use of Service[c]	
	(N)	(%)	(N)	(%)
Medical/Dental	115	94	107	93
Recreational	82	67	63	77
Counseling Service	79	65	62	78
Special Education or Training	74	61	67	90
Legal Services	67	55	52	78
Income	51	42	46	90
Day Care	44	36	31	75
Employment Counseling or Training	43	35	22	51
Housing	35	29	20	57
Drug Abuse/Alcoholism	11	9	8	73
Homemaker	9	7	3	33

[a] Information was missing for some children (not exceeding 10 children per service).
[b] N = 122 children in 107 families.
[c] This information is based on the responses of those who indicated a need for a service and then used it. Percentages are based on those who needed each of the services.

member of the family of 74 of the children (61%). Of these 74, 67 (90%) received the needed service.

Legal services were considered to be a need by the caretakers of 67 (55%) of the children. Of these, 52 (78%) received legal assistance.

Income assistance was perceived as a need in the families of 51 (42%) of the children. Of these, 46 (90%) actually received assistance.

The caretakers of 44 children (36%) expressed a need for day care. Of these 44, 33 (75%) were getting the needed assistance.

The need for employment services, such as employment counseling or job training, was felt by caretakers of 43 children (35%), but only half of them (22) received the services.

Housing was thought to be a need by the caretakers of 35 of the children (29%), and was met for 20 of them (57%).

Drug abuse or alcoholism services were viewed by the caretakers of 11 children (9%) as being needed. Eight of them (73%) also indicated that the services had been received.

Homemaker services were needed by the caretakers of 9 children (7%). Three (33%) actually received the services.

Use of Services in Each Type of Permanent Home

Service information from Interview III was also examined for each type of permanent home. As shown in table 6, in all types of homes, the demand was greatest for medical and dental services. In addition, the caretakers of the majority of children in biological homes said that they needed help with income, counseling, special education, legal services, recreation, employment training or counseling, and housing. A high proportion of caretakers of children in relatives' homes also expressed a need for service in most of these areas.

On the other hand, less than half of caretakers of the children in adoptive homes felt the need for legal services, special education, counseling, day care, and employment training or counseling. However, 71% of these caretakers indicated a need for recreational services.

Overall, parents in the biological homes expressed the greatest need for a variety of services, ranging from counseling to recreation to housing. This group expressed the need for help with daily living tasks (employment, housing, and income), along with less tangible aid, such as counseling and special education. Whereas the biological parents focused on a variety of concerns, caretakers in the other four permanent placement groups placed less emphasis on the basic areas of housing, employment, and income.

Relationship Between Stressful Life Events and Service Use

In the literature, a relationship has been suggested between the functioning of families and the number of stressful life events that they experience. Stressful events include illness or death of a family member, loss of a job, child expelled from school, and so forth [Antonovsky 1979, Monat and Lazarus 1977].

In the study reported here, caretakers were asked a number of questions about the life events that they or other family members had experienced around the time of the interviews (see fig. 1). The average number of life events reported was 2.3 at Interview I, 2.9 at Interview II, and 3.3 at Interview III.

Services used frequently enough to permit an analysis of their relation to life events were family or individual counseling, employment counseling or training, recreational services (e.g., Y.M.C.A., day camp), and special education. For each service, the sample was divided into two groups, one that used the service at some time during the study period and the other that did

TABLE 6 Need for Service in Each Type of Permanent Home (at Interview III)

Biological Homes (N = 51)	(%)	Adoptive Homes (N = 38)	(%)	Permanent Foster Homes (N = 12)	(%)	Relatives' Homes (N = 8)	(%)	Foster Parent Adoptive Homes (N = 13)	(%)
Medical/Dental	92	Medical/Dental	97	Medical/Dental	83	Medical/Dental	100	Medical/Dental	100
Income	82	Recreation	71	Counseling	83	Legal Services	88	Counseling	62
Counseling	76	Legal Services	47	Recreation	75	Counseling	75	Recreation	62
Special Education	72	Special Education	42	Special Education	75	Recreation	75	Day Care	46
Legal Services	67	Counseling	39	Legal Services	42	Special Education	62	Special Education	46
Recreation	63	Day Care	39	Day Care	25	Income	38	Employment Training/ Counseling	31
Employment Training/ Counseling	61	Employment Training/ Counseling	13	Income	17	Housing	38	Legal Services	23
Housing	57			Employment Training/ Counseling	17	Drug Abuse/Alcohol	25	Income	15
Day Care	39			Drug Abuse/Alcohol	17	Employment Training/ Counseling	12		
Homemaker	14								
Drug Abuse/Alcohol	12								

Each N refers to the number of children in each type of permanent home.

Figure 1   List of Stressful Life Events Discussed in the Interview with Parents or Caretakers

Started school
Graduated from school
Failed school
Expelled or suspended from school
Changed schools
Had a serious physical illness, injury, accident, hospitalization
Had frequent minor illnesses
Began psychotherapy, counseling, A.A., Synanon
Became pregnant
Lost a child through miscarriage or abortion
Gave birth to or adopted a child
Began work
Changed jobs or status (promoted, demoted)
Laid off temporarily, fired, quit (which one?)
Retired
Had an increase in financial status (money, property)
Had a loss of money, property
Was involved in legal action, gone to court, been arrested or jailed (not related to speeding or
    parking offenses or the signing of legal documents) (who was involved?)
Married
Separated, divorced, or had major marital problems (which one?)
Death of a close family member (may include former spouse)
Had a close friend move away or had a close friendship end

In the last few weeks,
Has your family moved?
Has a new person moved into your household other than (child's name)?

not. T tests of significance were employed to determine whether the two groups differed in the cumulative number of events experienced at any time during the study period. In addition, for those cases in which the service had been used at some time during the study period, correlational analysis was used to determine the relationship between the number of stressful life events and service use within the first 6 months.

As can be seen from table 7, the families that used individual or family counseling, employment counseling or training, and special education services experienced a higher number of stressful life events than those who did not use those services. Further, the correlations of the number of life events at each interview with the timing of service use, for those cases in which a service had been used, showed a number of significant relationships.

TABLE 7   Stressful Life Events and Use of Services

Services	Number of Families	Mean Number of Life Events	t-Value	Degrees of Freedom
Counseling				
Used counseling	62	7.4	−4.48**	115
Did not use counseling	55	4.9		
Employment				
Used employment service	22	8.8	−4.69**	115
Did not use employment service	94	5.6		
Recreation				
Used recreational service	62	6.7	−1.52*	115
Did not use recreational service	55	5.8		
Special Education				
Used special education	59	7.6	−5.06**	115
Did not use special education	58	4.8		

* $t < .05$.
** $t < .01$.

There was a correlation between the number of events at Interviews I and II and the use of counseling within the first 6 months after the child was placed. In addition, those families that experienced a large number of events at all interview times also tended to use employment counseling or training 7 to 13 months after the child was placed. Similarly, those that experienced a large number of stressful life events at Interview III tended to be those using recreational services 7 to 13 months after the child's placement. There was, however, no correlation between the number of events and timing of the use of special education services.

7. Infants and Toddlers

Forty-nine children whose ages ranged between 1 month and 2½ years were part of the study sample at Interview I. Many questions in the interview were not applicable to caretakers with children in this age group (e.g., Do you think this child expects to stay here?). As a result, a number of outcome items could not be answered by these caretakers. The infants and toddlers for whom a minimum number of questions could be answered, and who thus had outcome scores that could be computed, made up a group whose mean scores for those questions were much higher than the other age groups. With the complications of missing scores, ceiling effects, and significant differences between infants and toddlers and other age groups, it was necessary to treat the infants and toddlers as a separate sample rather than include them in the main analysis. Only descriptive information is therefore provided regarding the characteristics of these children, their placement histories, and the characteristics of their permanent families.

There were 20 children (41%) returned to their biological homes, 26 placed in adoptive homes (53%), 1 placed with relatives (2%), and 2 adopted by foster parents (4%). Most of the descriptive information that follows concentrates on the children returned to their biological homes and those who were adopted, since there were so few children in the other types of permanent homes (i.e., relatives and foster parent adoption).

Characteristics of the Children

Sixty-five percent of the infants and toddlers were male and 35% were female, as in the total study sample. The same percentages of males and females were returned to their biological homes and to adoptive homes. The majority of children in adoptive homes (81%) were 1 to 12 months old, with boys and girls equally represented. The children returned to their biological homes were from all age ranges; those 1 to 12 months old were mainly boys. The adopted children aged 12 to 24 months old were all girls.

Seventy-five percent of the infants and toddlers were white, 18% black, and 6% Hispanic or mixed racial background. Ninety-two percent of the adopted children were white and 65% of the children returned to their biological parents were white, 25% black, and 10% mixed race.

Placement History

In general, these children had little opportunity to develop extensive placement histories. Despite their young age, however, 27% had had more than one temporary placement in foster care. More specifically, 35% of the children who were returned to their biological homes and 19% of the adopted children had had more than one temporary placement. All of the children had been in at least one temporary foster home prior to the permanent placement. For 2 children, the foster parents had been relatives. Slightly more than one-third were in care up to 90 days, another third were in care from 3 to 6 months, and the remainder were in care from 6 months to over 2 years. The average age was 6 months. Those returned to biological homes had been in care an average of 5 months. The average time in care for adopted children was 6 months.

For all 49 children, the following were the most frequently cited reasons for placement in foster care:

1. the mother, who was not married, placed the child (35% of the children);

2. the parent was unwilling to care for the child (18%);

3. child neglect (14%);

4. unsuitable living conditions (14%);

5. child abuse (12%).

Often, more than one reason for placement was given. For children returned to their biological families, child neglect was the most frequently cited reason for foster care, followed by unsuitable living conditions, abuse, and family problems. For adopted children, the two main reasons for foster placement were "unwed mothers placing children," and "parents unwilling to care for their children."

When the length of time that caseworkers spent planning for the case was examined, differences were found in relation to the type of permanent home into which the child was placed. Both total planning time and the proportion of time spent planning in relation to the time the child was in temporary placement were greater for children in adoption than for children returned to their biological homes.

Characteristics of Permanent Families

Twelve of the children who returned to their biological families went back to single parents who had no other adults in the home (60%), 6 to single parents with other adults in the household (30%), and 2 to married biological parents (10%). Children in all other placements were placed with married couples. The average age of the biological parents interviewed was 23 years, that of the adoptive parents was 33 years.

A higher percentage of children in adoptive homes than those who returned to their biological families had no other child in the home. Thirty-five percent of those returned to their biological families had 3 or more children in the home, while only 15% of those adopted had 3 or more.

Twenty percent of the 49 families reported no stressful life events around the time of the interview. This was true for 25% of the biological families and 20% of the adoptive families. Forty percent of the families had had only one stressful event. Twenty-five percent of the biological parents, however, had experienced three or more stressful events around the time that the child was returned to them; only 11% of the adoptive families had had that many.

Approximately equal percentages of biological parents (20%) and adoptive parents (23%) indicated that they had no supports such as relatives, friends, or organizations available to them. Thirty-five percent of the biological parents had three or more such supports and 50% of the adoptive parents had that many.

Four of the biological parents (20%) said that they had barriers to service use, mainly transportation, money, and babysitting. Two adoptive parents mentioned barriers, including being unaware of services.

Information about contact between the caseworker and the parent at each interview time demonstrated that caseworker contact was high but varied by the type of permanent home. At Interview I, caseworkers had had contact with 85% of the families of children returned to their biological homes; this decreased to 50% by Interview III. At Interview I, caseworkers had had contact with 73% of the adoptive families and 80% of these families by Interview III. No second interviews were completed for 7 of the 20 children (35%) returned to biological homes, and no third interviews for an additional 4.

8. Descriptions and Comparisons of Children in Each Type of Permanent Home

This section contains descriptions of all the children in the study sample in each type of permanent home. It also includes comparisons of children in biological and adoptive homes, the two largest groups in the study sample. The information came from more than one source. Child characteristics, number of supports, and stressful life events were obtained from interviews with the caretakers in the permanent homes. Placement history and planning activity data were obtained from the case records and interviews with caseworkers approximately 1 to 6 months after the placement.

Biological Homes

Sex, Age, and Race of Children

One hundred children (53%) of the 187 in the study sample had been returned to their biological homes. Sixty-eight (68%) were boys. There were 10 sets of siblings.

The children returned to their biological homes did not cluster in any one age range; however, approximately 40% of all the children were under 6 years of age.

More of the black, Hispanic, and mixed race children were returned to their biological homes than white children. The non-whites, however, represent only 25% of the sample.

Age and Family Status of Biological Parents

The average age of biological parents was 31 years. Their marital status was diverse; over one-third (36) of this group were divorced, one-fourth (25) were married, 20 were separated, 18 were never married, and one was widowed. Of the 75 biological parents who were not presently married and living with their spouses, 22 (29%) had other adults living in the home and 53 (71%) had no other person over the age of 18 in the home. Of those who were separated, 85% had no other adult in the home; of those who were divorced, 71% had no other adult in the home; and of those who had never been married, 50% had no other adult in the home.

There was an average of 2.5 children living in the biological homes, including the child in the study.

Placement History

Children returned to their biological families had been in temporary care an average of 16 months since their most recent case openings, with 1.8 placements. Twenty percent had returned home previously.

More than one reason often was given for the child's placement in foster care. The most frequently cited reason for placement for children returned to their biological homes was neglect, followed by unsuitable living conditions, child's emotional problems, and abuse. Abandonment and the mother being unmarried and unwilling to assume care were cited least often. When neglect was one of the reasons for placement, the child's average time in care was over 2 years (27 months), with a mean of 2.3 placements; for abuse, it was 17 months, with a mean of 2.5 placements. When the child's emotional problems was one of the reasons, the average time in placement was 19 months, with 1.9 placements; for unsuitable living conditions, 15 months, with 1.3 placements. Most of the children (73%) had been in a non-relative foster home immediately prior to the permanent placement, but 17% had been in residential care and 10% in foster placements with relatives.

Eighty-four percent of the children returned to their biological homes had been visited by their biological parents while in temporary foster care.

Permanency Planning Activity

Information on the permanency planning done by the caseworkers was available for 95 of the 100 children returned to biological parents; for the others, the original plan was not completed and no planning information was available. Caseworkers spent an average of 5.8 months in planning.

Caseworkers felt that there was at least one system barrier to making permanent plans for children (e.g., lack of caseworker time, court and legal constraints, financial constraints, inability to get termination of parental rights) for 37% of the children; there were parent-related physical or emotional barriers for 64%; child-related barriers for 28%; and a negative relationship between parent and child, or sibling and child, for 19%. An inadequate home environment was a barrier for 45% of the children; inadequate supervision was a barrier for 26%.

Before the child was returned, services for emotional problems were received by 33% of the biological parents, services for the child's physical health were obtained for 31% of the children, and services for the child's emotional problems for 31%. Twenty-five children (25%) had been committed to the custody of the Commissioner of DCYS.

Caseworkers' contacts of some type (visit, phone call, or letter) after the child's return home occurred for 79 of the 100 children (79%) by Interview I, for 41 of the 71 children (58%) between Interviews I and II, and for 25 of the 51 children (49%) between Interviews II and III.

Disrupted Placements

Of the 62 children returned to their biological parents about whom there was information, 20 were no longer in the home by the end of the study. Fourteen were males, 6 were females. The average age was 9.1 years for the males and 4.7 years for the females. The previous placement of 9 children had been a foster home, 7 came from residential care, 2 from placements with relatives, and 2 from a permanent foster home.

Economic Status

The biological homes seemed to be at an economic disadvantage. Seventy-nine percent of the families had incomes of less than $10,000 per year, and many were in need of public assistance (82%) and public housing (57%).

Stressful Life Events and Social Supports

The biological families experienced an average of 2.5 stressful life events at Interview I, which was significantly more than adoptive families. This difference was maintained at Interviews II and III. In addition, the biological families used significantly fewer personal supports (e.g., friends, co-workers, parent groups) at Interviews I and II than adoptive families.

The barriers to the use of services cited most frequently by parents were lack of money or eligibility, transportation, and babysitting. Barriers were most frequently mentioned by parents who were separated from their spouses; next in frequency were by parents who were married, parents who were never married, and divorced parents.

Adoptive Homes

Sex, Age, and Race of Children

Forty-five children (24% of the sample) were placed in adoptive homes. Sixty percent were male, 40% female. Twenty-eight (62%) were under 3 years of age.

Almost all of the children in adoptive homes were white (91%); 3 were black (7%) and 1 was of mixed racial background (2%).

Age and Family Status of Adoptive Parents

The average age of adoptive parents was 33 years. Forty-three were married, 1 was divorced, and 1 was never married. The average number of children in the home was 2.1, including the study child.

Placement History

The children in adoptive homes had been in temporary foster care an average of 17.5 months since the most recent opening of their cases, with a mean of 2.5 placements. Twenty-two percent had been returned to their biological homes from foster care at least once and then re-entered temporary care. The most frequent reason for placement in foster care for this group was that the unmarried mother was unwilling to assume care of the newborn (38% of the children); the next most frequent reason was that a parent was unwilling to provide care of a child other than a newborn (20%), followed by abuse (16%), and mental illness of the parent (13%). (More than one reason for placement was sometimes given.)

For children placed because an unmarried mother was unwilling to assume care, the average time in care was 4.5 months, with a mean of 1.2 placements; those placed because the mother was unwilling to care for an older child were in foster care an average of 13.5 months, with 1.8 placements. When one of the reasons for placement was abuse, the average was almost 3 years (31.5 months) in care, with 4.3 placements; if the reason was mental illness of the parent, it was almost 2 years (20.5 months) in care, with 3.2 placements.

The vast majority of children (87%) placed in adoptive homes had been in foster homes immediately prior to the permanent placement. Nine percent had been in residential care and 4% in an adoptive placement that had disrupted. Biological parental visiting while the child was in foster care had occurred in 29% of the cases.

Permanency Planning Activity

The average amount of time caseworkers spent in permanency planning activity for these children was 7.5 months. Caseworkers perceived that system barriers (e.g., caseworker's lack of time, court and legal constraints, financial considerations, inability to get termination of parental rights) existed for 17 children (38%), parent-related physical or emotional barriers for 4 (9%), child-related barriers for 13 (29%), and foster parent relationship barriers for 7 (16%).

Pre-placement activities for these children included obtaining services for physical health for 17 children and services for emotional problems for 8 children. Nineteen children (42%) had been committed to the custody of the Commissioner of DCYS. Thirty-nine of the children were legally freed for adoption at the time the caseworkers were interviewed.

Caseworker contact after the child's placement in the adoptive home was made with 32 of the families (71%) by Interview I, 37 of the families (82%) between Interviews I and II, and 33 of the families (73%) between Interviews II and III. Although caseworker contact with children returned to biological homes decreased greatly over time, contact with children in adoptive placements was actually maintained or increased at Interviews II and III.

Disrupted Placements

Of the 39 children in adoptive homes about whom there was information, 1 child was no longer in the home by the end of the study.

Economic Status

All families had incomes over $10,000 a year.

Stressful Life Events and Social Supports

Adoptive families used significantly more personal supports at Interviews I and II and experienced fewer stressful life events by all interviews than biological families. The mean number of supports was 3.2 at Interview I, 2.6 at Interview II, and 3.1 at Interview III. The mean number of events was 1.9 at Interview I, 2.2 at Interview II, and 2.7 at Interview III.

Relatives' Homes

Sex, Age, and Race of Children

Fifteen children in the study sample (8%) had been placed with relatives on a permanent basis. Eight of the homes were with aunts, 6 were with grandmothers, and 1 was with a great-grandmother.

Seven of the children (47%) were male and 8 were female (53%). The average age of the children was 10.3 years. Almost half of the children (47%) were 12 years of age or older.

Eight of the children (53%) were white, 6 were black (40%), and 1 was of mixed racial background. There was 1 sibling set.

Age and Family Status of Relatives

The average age of caretakers who were relatives was 47 years. Their marital status varied: 6 (40%) were married, 3 widowed, 2 divorced, 2 separated, and 2 had never been married. Three of the 6 married couples had another adult, besides the spouse, living in the home. Eight of the 9 single relatives had at least one other adult in the home. There was an average of 2.7 children living in the home, including the study child.

Placement History

Children whose permanent placements were with relatives had been in temporary foster care for 1.6 years and had had an average of two placements. Only 15% had been returned home previously.

Abuse was the most frequently cited reason (47%) for the original placement in foster care, followed by neglect (29%) and family problems (21%). Most children (73%) had been in foster family care immediately before being placed with relatives; the other 27% had been in residential care.

Nine of the 15 children (60%) had been visited by the biological parents while in foster care, and 6 of the 15 were visited by parents in the current placement with relatives. Four were visited by other relatives.

Permanency Planning Activity

Information on caseworkers' planning activity was available for 14 of the 15 children; for 1 child the caseworker's plan was not accomplished and data were not obtained.

Caseworkers spent an average of 5 months in planning for these children. For 6 children (43%), caseworkers felt that there were system barriers— finances for 3 children and court and legal constraints for the other 3. The parents' social or emotional problems were seen as barriers for 6 other children, and the child's social or emotional problems were described as barriers to the placement plan for 4. Each of the following barriers was mentioned for 1 child: negative relationship with parent, inadequate home environment, and inadequate supervision.

Six of the children had received services for their physical health before the permanent placement, and 9 had received services for emotional problems. Four of the children (27%) were committed to the custody of the Commissioner of DCYS.

Caseworkers had contact with 80% of the children between the placement and Interview I, with 70% of the children between Interviews I and II, and with 100% of the children between Interviews II and III.

Disrupted Placements

Of the 10 children who were placed in relatives' homes, 2 were no longer in the home by the end of the study. Both were males over 12 years of age with special needs who returned to their biological families.

Economic Status

Sixty percent had incomes lower than $10,000 per year.

Stressful Life Events and Social Supports

These families tended to experience a relatively small number of stressful life events and also used the fewest supports of any type of permanent home. The average number of supports used by Interview III was 2.1, compared to as many as 5.4 for permanent foster families.

Permanent Foster Homes

Sex, Age, and Race of Children

For 14 children (7%), caseworkers made placements in foster homes with the intention that the placement be permanent, that is, that the children would stay there until they reached legal age. The majority of the children placed in permanent foster homes were male (78%). The mean age of the 14 children was 8.9 years. Thirteen of the children were white; 1 was black. There were 2 sets of siblings in the group.

Age and Family Status of Foster Parents

One permanent foster parent was widowed; the remainder were married. Their mean age was 41 years. Four families had at least one other adult in the home beside the parents, and they had an average of 3.1 children, including the study child.

Placement History

The children in this group had spent an average of 4.1 years in foster care, with a mean of 3.7 placements. Two (14%) had been returned to their biological parents previously.

Most frequently cited reasons for placement in foster care were abandonment by the parent (43%) and neglect (43%). Mental illness of the parent and family problems were also given as reasons for approximately 20% of the children.

Forty-three percent of the children had been in foster homes immediately prior to the permanent placement; another 43% had been in residential care (including one in a group home). Fourteen percent had been in foster care with a relative.

Parental visiting while the child was in temporary foster care occurred for 57% of the children; parental visiting in the permanent placement occurred for 14%. Fifty percent of the children also were visited by relatives.

Permanency Planning Activity

Information on amount of time spent by caseworkers in planning was available for 10 of the 14 children. For these 10 children, the average planning time was less than 3 months.

When caseworkers were asked about barriers to their plans, they indicated that there was only one child for whom system barriers (finances, time, legal issues) existed. Barriers related to the parent existed for three children, while half of the children had social or emotional problems that were viewed as barriers. For 3 children, a negative relationship between biological parent and child was seen as a barrier.

Six of the children had received services for their physical health prior to the permanent placement. Eight received services for emotional problems. Ten of the children (71%) were committed to the custody of the Commissioner of DCYS.

Caseworkers had been in contact with 64% of the children by Interview I, 92% between Interviews I and II, and 100% between Interviews II and III.

Disrupted Placements

Of the 14 children in permanent foster homes about whom there was information, 7 were no longer in the home by the end of the study. Two had left by Interview II and 5 by Interview III. The first two involved older males whose previous placements had been in residential care. In the five placements that disrupted by Interview III, 4 children were males, 1 female. All were 9 years of age or older. One had come from residential care. For at least 1 of these children, the foster parent did not view the placement as permanent although the caseworker did.

Stressful Life Events and Social Supports

By Interview I, permanent foster homes used an average of 2.9 personal supports and they had an average of 1.8 stressful life events.

Economic Status

Eighty-six percent had incomes higher than $10,000 per year.

Foster Parent Adoptive Homes

Sex, Age, and Race of Children

Although most children in the study physically moved from temporary care into permanent homes, one group of 13 children experienced only a change in status. They had been placed temporarily in the foster home and, after being there for a while, with the caseworkers' approval, were adopted by the foster parents. Seven of the children were male; 6 were female. Sixty-two percent were 5 years old or younger. Ten of the children were white, 1 black, 1 Hispanic, and 1 of mixed racial background. There were 2 sets of siblings.

Age and Family Status of Foster Parents

The mean age of the foster parents was 42 years. All of the parents were married couples; 5 had other adults living in the home as well. There was an average of 4.4 children living in the home, ranging in number from 2 to 9, including the study child.

Placement History

The children had been in foster care an average of 2.3 years, including time spent in the current home. Twenty-three percent had returned to their biological homes since the most recent opening of their cases and prior to the permanent placement. There was a wide variety of reasons for their placements in foster care, with unwed mothers placing their children (23%) and abuse (23%) as the two most frequent.

Five of the children had received services for their physical health as part of the caseworkers' activities prior to the permanent placement. Four had received services for their emotional problems. Eight (62%) were committed to the custody of the Commissioner of DCYS at the time the decision to adopt was made.

Permanency Planning Activity

Caseworkers spent an average of 5.3 months planning for the permanent placement. System barriers to the plan (e.g., caseworkers' lack of time, financial considerations, court and legal constraints, inability to get termination of parental rights) occurred for 69% of the children, with difficulty in terminating parental rights the most frequent. Emotional problems of the biological parents constituted a barrier for 54% of the children as well.

Only 1 of the 13 children presented individual problems that were seen by the caseworker as a barrier to the placement. One sibling set had a negative relationship with the biological parents, which was considered a barrier to placement.

Seven children had been visited by their biological parents while in foster care. After the decision to adopt was made, 5 still were visited by parents and 3 were visited by other relatives.

Caseworkers had been in contact with all children at Interviews I and II. Four children did not have contact with caseworkers between Interviews II and III.

Disrupted Placements

There were no disruptions of placements in this group.

Economic Status

Ninety-two percent had incomes higher than $10,000 per year.

Stressful Life Events and Social Supports

Fóster parent adoptive families experienced an average of 2.3 stressful life events. They used 1.6 personal supports.

Comparisons of Children in Biological and Adoptive Homes

Certain differences were found between children returned to their biological homes and children placed in adoptive homes. The most frequent reason for placement of children returned to their biological homes was neglect, whereas for children in adoptive homes it was "unmarried mothers unwilling to care for their children." Children returned to their biological homes had had fewer temporary placements than adopted children. More of the children returned to their biological homes than adopted children had been visited by their biological parents while in foster care.

Caseworker contact after placement also differed. Caseworkers had contact with significantly more adoptive families than with biological parents by Interviews II and III.

The number of personal supports was higher for adoptive families than for biological families at Interviews I and III and the mean number of stressful life events was lower for adoptive than biological families at all interview periods.

Almost all children (91%) in adoptive homes were white; 3 (7%) were black, and 1 (2%) was of mixed racial background.

9. Disrupted Placements

Contained here is information obtained from interviews carried out after disruption occurred, as well as from Interview I.

Of the 138 children whose whereabouts were known by the end of the study, 30 (22%) had left the permanent homes into which they had been placed. Sixteen of these disruptions occurred by Interview II (6 to 10 months from the permanent placement date), and 14 occurred by Interview III (12 to 16 months from the permanent placement date).

It is difficult to predict whether this rate of disruption will continue, whether it has peaked, or whether it will increase. In addition, a few of the disrupted placements of children returned to their biological homes may turn out to be temporary; in three of these situations, children whose placements had disrupted went back to their permanent homes by the end of the study.

Characteristics of Children and Permanent Homes

Of the 62 children returned to their biological homes about whom there was information at the end of the study, 20 (32%) had disrupted placements; of the 14 who were placed in permanent foster homes, 7 (50%) had disrupted placements. The remaining disrupted placements involved relatives' homes (2) and an adoptive home.

Twenty-three of the children (77%) were male; 7 were female. Eighteen (60%) were 9 years of age or older. Sixteen (53%) were boys 9 years of age or older (see table 8).

Twenty-two of the children (73%) were white, 7 were black (23%), and 1 was of mixed racial background. There were 2 sets of siblings whose placements disrupted.

The average age of the caretakers in the disrupted placements was 35 years (31 years for disruptions by Interview II, 39 years for disruptions by Interview III). Thirteen of the parents were married, 10 were divorced, 4 were separated, 2 were never married, and 1 was widowed. Over half (57%), therefore, were single parents. Nine of the parents (30%) had no other adults living in the home. For children returned to their biological homes, the percentage of single-parent placements that disrupted was similar to their representations in the sample—75% of all the biological families were single

TABLE 8   Age (at Permanent Placement) and Sex of Children Whose Placements Disrupted

Sex			Age			
	Under 3 Years	3–5 Years	6–8 Years	9–11 Years	12+ Years	Total
Male	1	3	3	5	11	23
Female	2	2	1	1	1	7
Total	3	5	4	6	12	30

parents and 70% of the disruptions in biological homes were single-parent families.

Placement History

For 13 (43%) of the children whose placements disrupted, caseworkers had given more than one reason for the child's previous entry into foster care. In the overall sample, however, multiple reasons were given for only 21% of the children. Neglect was one of the reasons for placement for 11 children (37%), abuse was a reason for 9 of the children (30%), and abandonment was a reason in another 7 (23%). Other reasons included family problems (6 children), mental illness of parent (5 children), and child's emotional or behavioral problems (5 children).

The children whose placements disrupted did not have a significantly higher number of previous foster placements than the 108 children whose placements did not disrupt and whose whereabouts were known at Interview III. Those whose placements disrupted by Interview II had had an average of 2.9 placements; those whose placements disrupted between Interview II and Interview III had had an average of 2.2 placements. The children in placements that disrupted by Interview II had spent an average of 19.5 months in temporary foster care; this figure is comparable for the children whose placements had not disrupted by Interview II, who had been in care an average of 22 months. The children whose placements disrupted between Interviews II and III had spent an average of 44 months in their most recent foster care placement. For the total number of children whose placements disrupted by the end of the study, the average time spent in foster care was 32 months. This was significantly higher than the average of 21 months for those whose placements had not disrupted. Children whose previous placements were in

TABLE 9   Placement History of Children Whose Placements Disrupted

Previous Placement	Average Number of Placements	Average Time in Care (in years)
Residential (*N* = 10)	4.2	5.3
Foster Family (*N* = 20)	1.8	1.3

residential care accounted for the most time in care and the greatest number of foster placements (see table 9).

Fifteen of the children (50%) whose placements disrupted had been in non-relative foster homes immediately prior to the permanent placement, 11 (37%) in residential care, 2 (7%) with relatives, and 2 (7%) in permanent foster homes. The 20 children whose placements disrupted and who had been in foster homes constituted 13% of the 154 children in the study sample who had come from foster homes; the 10 children who had been in residential care represented 32% of the 31 children in the study sample who had come from residential care.

One of the variables identified earlier as contributing significantly to outcomes was whether children had previously been returned to their biological homes from foster care. Regarding this variable, there was no significant difference between the children whose placements disrupted and those whose placements did not.

Biological parents for 23 children had visited their children in foster care prior to the permanent placement. Of the children who were visited were 16 of the 20 children who had been returned to their biological homes, 4 of the 5 children in permanent foster homes for whom there is information, both of the children who had been placed with relatives, and the child who had been adopted.

Permanency Planning Activity

Two children had disrupted placements for which the caseworkers' plans had not been accomplished. For 1 child, for whom the plan was for permanent foster care, the child actually went to live with a relative, the placement disrupted, and the child subsequently returned to the biological parent. For the other child whose plan was for placement in a residential treatment facility, the child actually went to the biological home, and after that placement disrupted, went to residential care.

The permanent plan was accomplished for the other 28 children, and information was available about barriers to the plan's completion and about the pre-placement services used. In 63% of the total disruptions (and 80% of the disruptions from the biological homes), a biological parent's emotional or social problems were seen by the caseworker as barriers to the placement. Child barriers (emotional or behavioral) were indicated in half of the placements that disrupted. For 7 children (23%), finances were mentioned as a barrier; for 5 (17%), caseworkers' lack of time was a barrier. Caseworkers felt that a negative relationship between a parent or sibling and the child was a barrier for 3 children returned to biological homes; an inadequate environment was described as a barrier for 5 children returned to their biological homes; inadequate supervision was seen as a barrier for 7 children returned to their biological homes.

The most frequently used pre-placement services for families in which disruptions of placements later occurred were for the child's emotional problems (15 children); services for parents' emotional problems were used by families of 12 children. Ten children received services for their physical health but it is not known whether these were routine or special services.

At Interview I, caseworkers had had contact with 23 children and no contact with 3. (Information was missing for 4 children.) The caseworkers had maintained contact with 8 of the 14 children who were still in permanent homes at the time of Interview II.

Reasons for Disruptions

For 11 children, the reasons given by caretakers for children's exit from the home were mainly the children's behavior problems, including trouble in school or with the law. For the other 5 children for whom interviews were completed and information given by the caretakers, reasons were that the child was living with the biological mother (although there was no indication whether this was a planned move), the child needed special residential care for medical and learning problems, the child was a victim of suspected abuse by the caretaker, the caretaker could not accept the child's problems, and the child left permanent foster care when a relative decided to adopt the child.

One explanation that has been suggested for disruptions in permanent homes is that families become vulnerable under stress and do not have adequate support systems or services to help them through the critical times.

In an effort to determine the vulnerability of these families and their use of support systems, the number of stressful life events they experienced and the sources of support they used were examined. The families of the 30 children whose placements disrupted had an average of 2.4 stressful events at Interview I. This was not significantly different from the 2.1 stressful events reported by families in which there were no disruptions.

Use of Supports and Services

Families with disrupted placements used on the average a similar number of personal supports as families with no disrupted placements. According to the 16 caretakers who had interviews after placements disrupted, social workers were one of the most helpful supports (for 15 children), followed by friends (for 5 children), community groups (for 4 children), and relatives (for 5 children in 3 families).

Seventeen of the 30 families with disrupted placements used counseling services; 6 of the disrupted families indicated a need for some type of counseling, although they did not use it; 4 listed barriers to the use of counseling, mostly money. Two said they did not need counseling but used it anyway. Nine families used recreational services and 7 felt the need but did not use the services; 4 mentioned a variety of barriers. Five felt the need for public housing but did not use it; 2 needed special education services but did not use them.

When the 30 caretakers were asked about barriers to service use in Interview I, 7 (23%) identified transportation as a problem, 9 (30%) felt lack of money or eligibility prevented service use, and 2 (7%) felt that the need for babysitters was a barrier. In subsequent interviews, transportation and money were mentioned by additional caretakers.

Services that would have been most used if barriers had not existed were recreational services and employment counseling or job training. Day care was mentioned less often.

Outcomes

The 30 children whose placements disrupted scored significantly lower on the Emotional and Developmental Functioning, School Functioning, and Family Adjustment outcome measures at Interview I, as compared to the 108 children who remained in their permanent homes. Whether these low scores represent an early predictor of disruption or only a passing symptom of what is occurring in a child's life cannot be determined. There was no significant difference on the Child Behavior outcome measures.

10. Summary of Findings

Information on the foster child's functioning and adjustment after placement in a permanent home was sparse until recently, with the possible exception of studies of adoptions, which were frequently retrospective. In the 1970s, Fanshel and Shinn's [1978] research and the Oregon Project [Lahti et al. 1978, Lahti and Dvorak 1981] began to fill some of the gaps. These led to other investigations, including the present one, that were designed to answer questions about children who leave foster care to enter homes that are considered permanent.

Child & Family Services of Hartford, CT, through funding from the U.S. Department of Health and Human Services, and in collaboration with the Connecticut Department of Children and Youth Services (DCYS) and The University of Connecticut School of Social Work, carried out this longitudinal study in a typical public child welfare setting, without special resources or focus on a particular group of children. The overall purpose of the research was to examine the effects of permanency planning. It was a study of 187 children under 14 years of age who had been in DCYS foster care for at least 30 days and were then placed in one of the following types of permanent homes: (1) biological, (2) adoptive, (3) relatives', (4) permanent foster, or (5) foster parent adoptive.

The children's parents or caretakers were interviewed three times (up to 4 months after placement, 6 to 10 months after placement, and 12 to 16 months after placement) over a 12- to 16-month period from the date of the permanent placement. Their case records were read and their caseworkers were interviewed. The findings are summarized here in relation to each of the study questions.

Which Children Leave Foster Care and Where Do They Go?

The children in the study sample came mostly from foster family care, although some (17%) came from residential care. The 2½- to 14-year-olds had been in foster care for an average of 24.8 months, with 2.3 previous placements. Those up to 2½ years old were a different group in many respects. They had an average of 6 months in foster care and significantly higher outcome scores. The most frequently cited reasons for placement for all children were abuse and neglect, but family problems, child behavior, unsuitable living conditions, and an unmarried mother unwilling to assume care were mentioned often.

The majority of children were returned to their biological parents. More males were placed in permanent homes than females (2 to 1). Children of all age groups were placed, but the majority of children in biological, permanent foster, and relatives' homes were 6 years or older; the majority of children in adoptive and foster parent adoptive homes were under 6 years of age. Forty-eight percent of the white children were placed in biological homes and 29% went to adoptive homes; among the black children, 66% went to biological homes and 9% to adoption. The Hispanic children were most often returned to their biological homes (86%).

Do These Children Remain in Their Permanent Homes?

Of the 138 children whose whereabouts were known by the end of the study, 30 (22%) had left their permanent homes during the study period. At Interview II (6 to 10 months after placement in permanent homes), 16 of the placements had disrupted. At Interview III (12 to 16 months following placement), 14 additional placements had disrupted. The disruption rate of 22% is similar to that of previous studies [Claburn et al. 1977, Block 1981]. Further discussion of the children whose placements disrupted is included later under the heading "What Are the Characteristics, Histories, and Situations of Those Children Whose Placements Disrupted?"

How Well Were the Children Functioning?

Children, as perceived by their caretakers, were doing moderately well in Family Adjustment and somewhat less well but adequately in Emotional and Developmental Functioning. There were several characteristics of the children and the homes that showed strong positive or negative relationships to these outcomes. Children who were doing well in Family Adjustment and Emotional and Developmental Functioning tended to be younger and to have had fewer foster placements. Race was also related to outcome, with black children doing best on certain measures. In addition to fewer foster placements, other placement history variables were related to outcome. Children who had been returned to their biological homes from foster care in the past were doing better than those who had not; that is, children seemed to be doing better on their second chance at returning home or were doing better in other permanent homes if they had been returned to their biological homes at least once. Children also did better when they were placed in homes with certain characteristics: foster parent adoptive homes, parents who were married, family incomes over $10,000, or several children in the family.

The children were doing moderately well in School Functioning. At Interview I, School Functioning was related to the sex of the child, with females doing better. Certain placement history variables were also related to outcome: the number of foster care placements (those with fewer placements scored higher), the type of previous placement (those who had been in relatives' foster homes did best), and the number of returns to the biological home from foster care in the past (those who had been returned in the past scored higher). Children who were placed in adoptive homes also did better on the School Functioning outcome measure than those in other types of homes.

These findings indicate that a variety of factors are related to outcome after leaving foster care. The age of the child was found to be one of the major factors, as it was in the Oregon project and other studies [Fanshel and Shinn 1978, Lahti et al. 1978]. Children who were older seemed to be having more difficulty in making an adjustment when placed in their permanent homes, perhaps because older children may be less able to alter their fantasies about previous parental relationships even if the parent is not present or has undergone a number of changes since the child was last in the home. Older children also are moving toward independence rather than the dependent relationships that may be more gratifying to the caretakers in a new family situation.

The study analysis revealed that black children were doing best on certain measures at certain times, a finding which is in agreement with those of Jones, Neuman, and Shyne [1976]. It is not clear why this is so. Of the 32 black children placed, 21 (66%) were returned to their biological homes, 6 (19%) were placed with relatives, 3 (9%) in adoption, 1 in permanent foster care, and 1 in foster parent adoption. Their mean age was 6.8 years and most were male (78%). Twenty-two percent had previously been in residential care. They had been in care an average of almost 2 years, with 1.9 previous placements. Only 9% had been returned to their biological homes previously. Approximately one-fifth had multiple reasons for placement. The most frequently mentioned reasons for entering care were abuse (25%), unsuitable living conditions (19%), neglect (16%), child's emotional or behavioral problems (16%), and abandonment (12%). Almost 80% of the permanent families of black children had incomes less than $10,000. Eighty-one percent were single parents but 54% of these had another adult living in the home. Although black children and their families had characteristics such as fewer previous returns to their biological homes and lower incomes that were related to poorer outcome scores for the total study population, the findings indicated that they were doing better in some areas of functioning at some interview times than other children. Further study is needed to clarify the meaning of these findings.

In the total study sample, placement history was related to outcome not only in the analysis of all 2½- to 14-year olds but also in the comparison of children whose placements disrupted with those whose did not. It is not surprising that children with more foster placements were not doing as well as those with fewer placements. Number of placements is highly correlated with time in care, so these children had been in the foster care system longer. They did not experience the continuity of care that is generally considered paramount in a child's growth and functioning. They may have developed emotional problems over the course of several placements that interfered with a smooth adjustment, or they may not have been willing to invest themselves in one more placement when their past experience suggested it might be temporary. Although the Oregon project found that the number of past placements did not contribute significantly to outcome [Lahti et al. 1978], that project was working specifically with children of whom the majority had had a number of placements and were being placed in adoption—a very different sample from this study.

Other factors in the placement history also contributed to outcome in the present study. Children whose previous placements had been with relatives were doing better than children whose previous placements had been in non-relative foster homes or in residential care. Apparently, a child's adjustment can be facilitated by continued contact with the family, which may provide a tie to the biological parent or a greater sense of belonging. Caseworkers might examine more closely the possibility of temporary foster care placements with relatives, in light of this finding.

Another placement history variable associated with outcome was a previous return to the biological parent from foster care. Children who had been in foster care, and were subsequently placed in a permanent home of any type, were doing better than those who had not been returned home previously; this included children whose previous placement was their first and only foster placement. It is possible that children who experienced some continued contact with the biological parent, even though it was sometimes short-term, felt more connected with the biological home and therefore made an easier transition back into it (for children returned to their biological homes), or had the opportunity to experience living with their biological parents again and to realize that it would not work out well (for children placed in other types of permanent homes).

It is also possible that caseworkers spent more time and energy on the children who had already reentered the system at least once, since they may have viewed these children as more vulnerable. Some evidence for this hypothesis came from data on caseworker contact with families. Further study of this phenomenon should help to understand better the specific conditions under which a return to the biological home is useful.

Several characteristics of permanent homes were also related to outcome. The children whose foster parents decided to adopt were adjusting better than other children at all time periods. There were no disruptions of placements for this group of children. This is not surprising, since these children had been living in the home for some time prior to the decision to adopt, and their ability to get along in the family was probably a factor in the decision. This provides evidence for a continuing stability in this type of adoption that is encouraging. Somewhat less striking, but still positive, were the outcomes of children currently in placements with relatives. They also were adjusting better than children in other types of permanent homes, but the effect was statistically significant only at Interview I for Family Adjustment and Interview II for Child Behavior outcomes. When these data are added to the finding that children who had been in temporary care with relatives also were doing better in their subsequent permanent placements, the case for care by relatives is strengthened. There should be further exploration of the role of relatives as a placement resource [Grinnell and Jung 1981].

Higher incomes were associated with better outcomes, as in the Oregon study [Lahti et al. 1978]. This again may be a function of a family's need to have its basic requirements (housing, food, and clothing) met before its social and emotional needs, which are the focus of the outcome measures, can be given priority.

Children placed in homes with single parents who had no other adults living in the home were doing less well in Family Adjustment than those in two-parent families or single parents with at least one other adult in the home. This finding should be viewed in light of the general situation of the single parents in the study, many of whom had incomes less than $10,000 and a need for housing, and who were dealing with separation or divorce. The additional financial stress on the single-parent family may make it harder to meet the basic physical needs of the family and, in effect, may sap the time and energy required to satisfy the emotional needs of both the children and parents.

What Services Do Children and Their Families Need and Use and How Are They Related to Stressful Life Events?

Caretakers of almost all the 122 children in the third interview sample expressed a need for medical and dental services, two-thirds needed counseling services, and nearly two-thirds needed special education services. In approximately one-third of the families there was a need for financial assistance, employment counseling or training, and housing. The likelihood of fulfilling service needs was greatest for medical and dental services, special education or training, and financial assistance, and least for employment counseling or training and housing.

Parents of the children who returned to their biological homes expressed the need for the greatest variety of services. They indicated a desire for help both with basic daily needs (such as employment, housing, and income) and with the less tangible needs (such as counseling and special education services). The other four types of permanent homes (adoptive, permanent foster care, relatives' and foster parent adoptive) focused on concerns other than the basics of housing, employment, and income.

The families that used individual or family counseling, employment counseling or training, recreation, and special education services also experienced a greater number of stressful life events over the study period than those who did not use those services.

The timing of service use was related to the number of events at certain interview times. At Interviews I and II, there was a positive relationship between the use of counseling and the number of stressful life events; also the use of counseling services was more likely to begin during the first 6 months. Initiation of use of recreational services 7 to 13 months after the child's placement was also related to the number of events occurring at the time. In the use of employment services, however, those who had had more stressful life events at all interview times were more likely to have begun service use 7 to 13 months after the child's placement rather than immediately after.

The use of counseling and recreational services appears to have begun around the time that a number of stressful events were occurring; use of employment services was initiated later. Parents may have been more willing to seek early counseling help for emotional or school-related problems because they felt helpless to deal with them themselves, or they may have been prepared for the need for counseling and were referred in a timely fashion to an agency where it could begin.

The need for employment counseling or training services may be less prevalent at the beginning of placement because such a need may have followed a series of stressful events. In addition, the later use of employment counseling or training services may be a result of the perception that those services are less readily available or less apt to have a successful outcome.

What Are the Characteristics and Needs of the Different Types of Permanent Homes?

A profile of the children in each type of home follows, along with information about their specific needs and the characteristics of their families. It is important to remember that the number of children placed with relatives, in permanent foster homes, or with foster parents who decided to adopt is very small, limiting any generalization from the available information.

The children who returned to their biological homes were, by far, the most diverse group in terms of characteristics and placement history. The biological family as a unit tended to be the most vulnerable family, although the child within the permanent foster care home was the most vulnerable individual. Over half of the biological families had a need for basic services. They also had fewer personal supports than the adoptive families and experienced a greater number of stressful life events at all interview times than adoptive families. The parents' conditions or problems were often seen by caseworkers as barriers to placement. The majority of children returned to biological families were with single parents with no other adult in the home. Although being a single parent is no longer considered to be a great barrier to permanent placement, as it was in the past, it often involves difficulties such as less income or a need for day care or other supports.

The major needs of biological families and children, as perceived by the biological parents, were for medical and dental care, financial help, counseling, special education, legal services, recreation, employment, and housing. To relieve the multiple needs of these families, a variety of resources may have to be brought to bear—from financial, employment, or housing assistance, to such outlets as recreational services or babysitters, and, finally, help in emotional adjustment or functioning through counseling. The cost of meeting families' needs with a variety of resources must be weighed against the detrimental effects of children remaining in foster care for prolonged periods of time.

In some respects, children placed in adoptive families faced fewer difficulties, since these families experienced fewer stressful life events at all interview times and had more personal supports than biological families. Although the adopted children, with the exception of the very young group (up to 2½ years), had more extensive foster care histories and more foster placements which were associated with poorer outcomes overall, there was only one disruption within 1 year. Other studies have indicated higher disruption rates for adoptions [Fein et al. 1979], or that disruptions of this group may occur later in the placement. The commitment to adopt may contribute to the maintenance of the placement and to a longer trial period than for other types of permanent homes.

Children placed with relatives were likely to be female and older. The relatives were mostly single parents. The family's income was less than $10,000 per year in 60% of the cases. Caseworkers found that, in planning for many of these cases, they encountered system barriers such as financial considerations or court or legal constraints.

The study sample included only a small number of placements with relatives—too small for generalization. The fact that it was a small group, however, leads to speculation. Why were so few children placed with relatives in situations in which a return to biological parents was not possible? Was this choice explored? Are the difficulties encountered in this type of placement too great, with too much caseworker time or financial contributions on the part of the client involved? If so, how can placements with relatives be made more feasible?

The children placed in permanent foster homes were found to be among the most vulnerable and needy of the different groups of children. They were mostly older boys and had extensive placement histories, with an average of 3.7 placements. Forty-three percent of the children also had been in residential care immediately prior to the permanent placement. The children's social and emotional problems were perceived by the caseworkers as barriers to the permanent placement in half the cases. Half of the permanent foster placements disrupted, but the children that remained were doing satisfactorily, as measured by their outcome scores.

Although many of the permanent foster care children did not do well in their placements, those in the foster parent adoptive groups were doing extremely well. They excelled in outcome measures (Family Adjustment and Emotional and Developmental Functioning) and all were still in their permanent homes at Interview III. These children had been with their foster parents prior to the decision to adopt, and much of the adjustment may have already been made. Also, in this type of placement, both the child and the parents had had the opportunity to explore the possibility of a meaningful adjustment and had developed a relationship before the first research interview. In addition, the parents knew more about the child's strengths and vulnerabilities, and still decided to adopt, thus reflecting the strength of their commitment to the child.

What Are the Characteristics, Histories, and Situations of Those Children Whose Placements Disrupted?

Thirty of the 138 children whose whereabouts were known (22%) left their permanent homes within 12 to 16 months of placement. Thirty-two percent of the children who had returned to their biological homes and 50% of the children placed in permanent foster homes had disrupted placements. Sixteen of the 30 children (53%) were older boys (9 to 14 years), as compared to 72 of the 187 (38%) in the entire study.

These children had spent more time in temporary foster care than children who did not have disrupted placements, and many had been in residential care before the move into permanent homes. For 43% of these children, the caseworkers had listed multiple reasons for placement.

Families that had disrupted placements did not experience a significantly higher number of stressful life events, nor did they use a higher number of supports and services than families in non-disrupted placements. Several parents indicated, however, that they felt a need for some type of service, particularly counseling, but did not use it. Lack of transportation and money were frequently mentioned as barriers to service use.

In terms of outcome, the children did less well on the Emotional and Developmental Functioning, Family Adjustment, and School Functioning measures than those whose placements did not disrupt.

How Does a Caseworker's Permanency Planning Affect Outcome?

The study did not address the appropriateness of the permanent plan or the decision-making process, since the purpose was to explore what occurred *after* a placement decision was made. Caseworkers said that they had made plans for all of the 187 children in the study sample.

In 178 cases, the plan was accomplished and the child was placed in the permanent home. In the other 9 cases, the children were placed in other homes either because they returned to their biological or relatives' homes without the caseworkers' approval or because the children went to permanent foster homes rather than into adoption.

Two major limitations were encountered in the collection of planning data. First, case records did not contain information on the extent of the planning or the services provided to each child or family. Second, caseworkers had limited time for research interviews. As a result, data on use of pre-placement services and barriers to planning were available but it was not possible to obtain details on the frequency, timing, and reasons for the services.

The caseworker's perception of a negative relationship between parent or sibling and child was correlated with outcome. When a negative relationship was considered as a barrier by the caseworker, the child had poorer outcomes on the Family Adjustment measure at Interviews I and III and on the Emotional and Developmental Functioning and the Child Behavior measures at Interview III.

Although this study did not find that the particular planning variables examined, such as use of pre-placement services, had an effect on outcome, the importance of planning is not diminished. Other studies [Jones et al. 1976, Lahti et al. 1978] have found certain aspects of planning to be associated with outcomes of foster care. It is probable that the information obtained in this study was not detailed enough to be useful in demonstrating a relationship between planning and outcome.

11. Practice Considerations

This study of children who went into permanent placements following temporary foster care found that the majority were functioning well and continued to be in their permanent homes 12 to 16 months later. Since the study was exploratory in nature, did not follow the children for more than 16 months, and did not have a comparison group of children who remained in foster care, there should be caution in interpreting the findings and offering generalizations. A number of findings are sufficiently strong, however, to suggest implications that should be considered in continuing efforts to improve service delivery in behalf of children and their families, particularly in regard to the crucial area of aftercare.

Impact of Foster Care Placement

Children with more foster care placements scored significantly lower on the outcome measures of Emotional and Developmental Functioning than those with fewer placements. Although it is widely believed among child welfare professionals that a child who is moved from one foster placement to another (rather than having a more stable foster care environment) will function less well, this had not been previously demonstrated empirically in a large sample of children. This finding supports the importance of carefully exploring and evaluating what is the best initial placement for a child, hence avoiding re-placement.

Another pertinent finding was that children who had been returned to their biological homes from foster care in the past (and had been returned home again in this study or had been placed in another type of permanent home) were doing better in terms of Family Adjustment and Emotional and Developmental Functioning than those who had not. Yet, as Gruber [1978] reported in his study of foster children in Massachusetts, many children remain in foster care indefinitely and are not even returned to their parents for trial periods. Although the best interests of the child are always paramount, the findings of the present study suggest that agencies should not be overly wary of returning a child home, possibly on a trial basis, assuming that it is done carefully and planfully, with participants aware of its purpose. In addition to serving an evaluative purpose, such a return may provide opportunities for child and parents to test whether they can live together, to learn or relearn how to function together, to receive appropriate help from the caseworker or other community resources, and, ultimately, to confront more realistically whether an alternative permanent plan is indicated. Indeed there may be times when such a return home should be a requisite before adoptive placement, such as (1) to test whether the bond between biological parent and child, a supposed barrier to adoption, is indeed intact; or (2) to puncture fantasies about the biological home and to give a child the freedom to relate to a new family.

Roles of Relatives

It was also revealed in the study that children whose previous foster placements had been with relatives were doing better than those who had been in non-relative foster family care or in residential placements. In addition, children who were currently in permanent placements with relatives were doing better on a number of outcome measures than children in other types of permanent homes.

These results underscore the importance of relatives as a potential resource in any consideration of temporary or permanent placement. Relatives can play significant roles in supporting parents, as well as in helping children to maintain their sense of family identity, continuity, and human connectedness, factors severely undermined by separations from biological families [Laird 1979]. Black children's better outcome scores in the present study may be a function of the network of relatives often found in black families.

There is a need for greater attention, in research as well as in practice, to the significance of the kinship system in permanency planning. The role of relatives in permanency planning should be explored further, especially since the strengths and resources of the extended family among population groups such as blacks and Puerto Ricans are being increasingly recognized [Hall and King 1982, Hill 1971, Mizio and Delaney 1981, Walker 1981]. As suggested by writers on child welfare services with minority groups, the concept of permanency planning itself perhaps should be broadened to encompass placement with the extended family system rather than simply the nuclear family [Baran, Pannor, and Sorosky 1976; Ishisaka 1978; Walker 1981]. It is noteworthy that the federal Indian Child Welfare Act of 1978 (Public Law 95-608) mandates that when native American children cannot remain with their parents, priority be given to placement either with members of the child's extended family or with other members of the child's tribe.

Foster Parent Roles in Permanency Planning

Although the number of children in the sample who were adopted by foster parents was small, they were doing very well at all time periods, particularly in relation to their Family Adjustment. These children had been a part of the foster family before their inclusion in the study; their adjustment, therefore, had already begun and was probably a factor in the foster parents' decision to adopt.

Children in permanent foster homes, however, were vulnerable in several respects and needed special attention from a variety of sources. There was also a large number of disrupted placements in this group, although those children who remained in permanent foster care were doing adequately by the end of the study. Most children placed in permanent foster homes were over 6 years of age and had more previous foster care placements and a greater number of problems than other children in the sample. They were probably in permanent foster care because a return to biological parents or adoption were not good choices.

These findings do not necessarily mean that permanent foster care is not a valid choice in permanency planning. They do suggest the need to explore its significance further, in practice as in research. Perhaps permanent foster care is a contradiction in terms. Perhaps ways can be found to enhance the child's sense of permanence when placed in this type of home. At any rate, this choice should be carefully considered, in particular by assessing the types of children for whom it is suitable and the methods and services required to make it work for children who are especially vulnerable.

Biological Families

As noted by previous investigators [Fanshel 1981, Fanshel and Shinn 1978], biological families were found to be the most common resource for permanency planning for children in the study. At the same time, among all types of permanent homes, biological families were clearly the most vulnerable in a variety of key life areas. They had multiple family needs, particularly in basic needs such as housing, employment, and income.

A substantial proportion of the children, moreover, had been returned to single-parent families, which nearly always meant the mother. It is especially noteworthy that children of single parents who had no other adults in the home were not doing as well as children of married parents or single parents who had other adults living with them.

The vulnerability of biological families of children in foster care has been repeatedly emphasized by researchers and writers in child welfare [Fanshel and Shinn 1978, Jenkins and Sauber 1966, Maluccio and Sinanoglu 1981]. The findings of this study underscore the biological family's needs for comprehensive, systematic, and ongoing services, as stressed by the federal Adoption Assistance and Child Welfare Act of 1980 (Public Law 96-272) and increasingly recognized in the field of child welfare [Horejsi, Bertsch, and Clark 1981; Maluccio and Sinanoglu 1981; Sinanoglu and Maluccio 1981]. In addition, other themes emerge, such as the importance of caseworkers being especially sensitive to the needs of children reunited with single parents who have no other adult living with them and being aware of resources that can be mobilized to increase the family's level of adjustment despite the difficulties often associated with being a single parent.

Services and Supports

The study showed that many families, especially the biological families, were in need of the most basic services during the aftercare period. Many parents expressed their needs for housing, employment, and financial assistance, while workers tended to emphasize services such as counseling. Obviously, it is difficult for parents to meet the emotional needs of their children if they are worrying about shelter, food, and clothing. In these cases, caseworkers may be most helpful as case coordinators, in addition to providing counseling and other supports to the family. They may link families with other agencies that handle housing or financial problems, suggest job training, explore recreational opportunities for the children, inform the parents of the availability of special education services for a child, or make arrangements for the use of a Parent Aide. The caseworker's help may also be crucial to enable parents to identify, use, and build on informal supports that exist (or could be developed) within their social networks.

The findings indicated that caseworkers maintained contact with most adoptive parents at all interview times, while greatly decreasing contacts with biological families following return of the child to the home. In part, this was probably caused by the fact that adoption of a child, in general, does not become final for a year. In contrast, after a child is returned to the biological home, his or her case is often swiftly closed.

According to the study, adoptive families typically have more resources (such as higher incomes and two parents in the home) at their command than biological families. Yet adoptive families may require the specific support of the caseworker, who can help in the child's adjustment to the new family. In times of scarce funding, however, it is crucial to ensure that the neediest families, which often means biological families, also have sufficient contacts with caseworkers. Ideally, all "permanent" families in need should receive necessary attention and support. This is a policy matter that requires adequate staffing, worker cooperation, and close monitoring for successful implementation.

The findings related to services and supports suggested that service delivery should focus on the family unit, especially in relation to factors that may have contributed to placement and may still exist. Case coordination activities, as well as supports, could be valuable, particularly if aftercare is viewed as a means of preventing reentry into foster care. As argued by proponents of the ecological perspective on child welfare, interventive approaches should emphasize the removal of environmental pressures on families and the provision of appropriate supports to children and parents [Laird 1979, Maluccio 1981, Minuchin 1970]. This approach would require a number of policy and practice changes, such as an expanded role for caseworkers, emphasis on case coordination and management, provision of adequate supportive services, and encouragement of continued caseworker contact with biological families in the aftercare period, which in some cases may last for many years and even until the child reaches maturity.

The findings also indicated that recreation, in particular, should receive more attention than it generally does in practice. Following medical and dental services, recreational services were in high demand, along with counseling and special education, and many families used recreational programs. Recreation was mentioned frequently as one service that families would have used if barriers had not existed. Use of recreational programs was also related to the number of stressful life events experienced (i.e., a family with a high number of stressful life events was likely to use recreation). In a number of permanent placements that disrupted, the parents or caretakers specifically indicated that they needed recreational services but could not use them because of obstacles such as lack of transportation. In effect, recreational programs may temporarily alleviate some of the stresses facing family members and allow them to rebuild their resources or coping mechanisms.

Epilogue

As this study was being completed, the permanency planning movement gained further momentum at the national level through enactment of the Adoption Assistance and Child Welfare Act of 1980 (Public Law 96-272).

This landmark Act mandates states to provide the kinds of programs, such as home-based services and supports to biological parents, that were found to be important for the families in the study. The findings of the study are strikingly consistent with the thrust of the Act, and full implementation of its requirements is essential if life in a permanent family is to become a reality for the large number of children caught in the web of child welfare service delivery.   ◆

References

Antonovsky, Aaron. Health, Stress, and Coping. San Francisco, CA: Jossey-Bass, 1979.

Baran, Annette; Pannor, Reuben; and Sorosky, Arthur D. "Open Adoptions." Social Work 21 (March 1976): 97–100.

Block, Norman M. "Toward Reducing Recidivism in Foster Care." Child Welfare 60 (November 1981): 597–610.

Children's Defense Fund. Children Without Homes. Washington, D.C.: Children's Defense Fund, 1978.

Claburn, W. Eugene, and Magura, Stephen. "Administrative Case Review for Foster Children." Social Work Research & Abstracts 14 (Spring 1978): 34–40.

Claburn, W. Eugene; Magura, Stephen; and Chizeck, Susan P. "Case Reopening: An Emerging Issue in Child Welfare Services." Child Welfare 56 (December 1977): 655–663.

Claburn, W. Eugene; Magura, Stephen; and Resnick, William. "Periodic Review of Foster Care: A Brief National Assessment." Child Welfare 55 (June 1976): 395–405.

Downs, Susan W.; Bayless, Linda; Dreyer, Linda; Emlen, Arthur C.; Hardin, Mark; Heim, Lori; Lahti, Janet; Liedtke, Kathryn; Schimke, Karen; and Troychak, Mary. Foster Care Reform in the 70's—Final Report of the Permanency Planning Dissemination Project. Portland, OR: Regional Research Institute for Human Services, Portland State University, 1981.

Emlen, Arthur; Lahti, Janet; Downs, Glen; McKay, Alec; and Downs, Susan. Overcoming Barriers to Planning for Children in Foster Care. Portland, OR: Regional Research Institute for Human Services, Portland State University, 1977.

Fanshel, David. "Foreword," in The Challenge of Partnership: Working with Parents of Children in Foster Care, edited by Anthony N. Maluccio and Paula A. Sinanoglu. New York: Child Welfare League of America, 1981, ix–xi.

Fanshel, David. "The Exit of Children from Foster Care: An Interim Report." Child Welfare 50 (February 1971): 65–81.

Fanshel, David, and Shinn, Eugene B. Children in Foster Care—A Longitudinal Investigation. New York: Columbia University Press, 1978.

Fein, Edith; Davies, Linda; and Knight, Gerrie. "Placement Stability in Foster Care." Social Work 24 (March 1979): 156–157.

Gil, David. "Developing Routine Follow-Up Procedures for Child Welfare Services." Child Welfare 43 (May 1964): 229–240.

Grinnell, Richard M. Jr., and Jung, Sherri. "Children Placed with Relatives." Social Work Research & Abstracts 17 (Fall 1981): 31–32.

Gruber, Alan R. Children in Foster Care. New York: Human Sciences Press, 1978.

Hall, Ethel H., and King, Gloria C. "Working with the Strengths of Black Families." Child Welfare 61 (November/December 1982): 536–544.

Hill, Robert S. The Strengths of Black Families. New York: Emerson Hall Publishers, 1971.

Horejsi, Charles R.; Bertsche, Ann V.; and Clark, Frank W. Social Work Practices with Parents of Children in Foster Care. Springfield, IL: Charles C. Thomas, 1981.

Iowa Department of Social Services, Foster Care Research Project. Increasing the Effectiveness of Foster Care Through the Use of the Service Contract with Children, Natural Parents, Foster Parents and Workers. Mimeographed. Des Moines, IA: Iowa Department of Social Services, Division of Community Services, August 1977.

Ishisaka, Hideki. "American Indians and Foster Care: Cultural Factors and Separation." Child Welfare 57 (May 1978): 299–308.

Jenkins, Shirley. "Duration of Foster Care—Some Relevant Antecedent Variables." Child Welfare 46 (October 1967): 450–456.

Jenkins, Shirley, and Sauber, Mignon. Paths to Child Placement—Family Situations Prior to Foster Care. New York: Community Council of Greater New York, 1966.

Jones, Mary Ann; Neuman, Renee; and Shyne, Ann. A Second Chance for Families. New York: Child Welfare League of America, 1976.

Judd, Charles M., and Kenny, David A. Estimating the Effects of Social Interventions. Cambridge, England: Cambridge University Press, 1981.

Lahti, Janet, and Dvorak, Jacqueline. "Coming Home from Foster Care," in The Challenge of Partnership: Working with Parents of Children in Foster Care, edited by Anthony N. Maluccio and Paula A. Sinanoglu. New York: Child Welfare League of America, 1981, 52–66.

Lahti, Janet; Green, Karen; Emlen, Arthur; Zendry, Jerry; Clarkson, Quentin D.; Kuehnel, Marie; and Casciato, Jim. A Follow-Up Study of the Oregon Project. Portland, OR: Regional Research for Human Services, Portland State University, August 1978.

Laird, Joan. "An Ecological Approach to Child Welfare: Issues of Family Identity and Continuity," in Social Work Practice: People and Environments, edited by Carel B. Germain. New York: Columbia University Press, 1979, 174–209.

Maas, Henry S., and Engler, Richard E. Children in Need of Parents. New York: Columbia University Press, 1959.

Magura, Stephen, and Claburn, W. Eugene. "Foster Care Review: A Critique of Concept and Method." Journal of Social Welfare 5 (Summer 1978): 25–34.

Maluccio, Anthony, and Fein, Edith. "Permanency Planning Revisited," in Foster Care: Current Issues and Practices, edited by Martha Cox and Roger Cox. Northwood, NJ: Ablex Press, 1983a.

Maluccio, Anthony N., and Fein, Edith. "Permanency Planning: A Redefinition." Child Welfare 62 (May/June 1983b): 95–201.

Maluccio, Anthony N., and Sinanoglu, Paula A., eds. The Challenge of Partnership: Working with Parents of Children in Foster Care. New York: Child Welfare League of America, 1981.

Maluccio, Anthony N. "An Ecological Perspective on Practice with Parents of Children in Foster Care," in The Challenge of Partnership: Working with Parents of Children in Foster Care, edited by Anthony N. Maluccio and Paula A. Sinanoglu. New York: Child Welfare League of America, 1981, 22–35.

Maluccio, Anthony N.; Fein, Edith; Hamilton, V. Jane; Klier, JoLynne; and Ward, Darryl. "Beyond Permanency Planning." Child Welfare 59 (November 1980): 515–530.

Meier, Elizabeth. "Current Circumstances of Former Foster Children." Child Welfare (April 1965): 192–206.

Minuchin, Salvador. "The Plight of the Poverty-Stricken Family in the United States." Child Welfare 49 (March 1970): 124–130.

Mizio, Emelicia, and Delaney, Anita J. Training for Service Delivery to Minority Clients. New York: Family Service Association of America, 1981.

Monat, Alan, and Lazarus, Richard S., eds. Stress and Coping—An Anthology. New York: Columbia University Press, 1977.

Murphy, H.B.M. "Predicting Duration of Foster Care." Child Welfare 47 (February 1968): 76–84.

Pike, Victor; Downs, Susan; Emlen, Arthur; Downs, Glen; and Case, Denise. Permanent Planning for Children in Foster Care: A Handbook for Social Workers. Publication No. (OHDS) 78-30124. Washington, D.C.: Department of Health, Education, and Welfare, 1977.

Regional Research Institute for Human Services. Barriers to Planning for Children in Foster Care. Vol. 1. Portland, OR: Regional Research Institute for Human Services, Portland State University, 1976.

Rooney, Ronald H. "Permanency Planning: Boon for All Children?" Social Work 27 (March 1982): 152–158.

Sherman, E.A.; Neuman, R.; and Shyne, A. Children Adrift in Foster Care. New York: Child Welfare League of America, 1973.

Sinanoglu, Paula A., and Maluccio, Anthony N., eds. Parents of Children in Placement: Perspectives and Programs. New York: Child Welfare League of America, 1981.

Stein, Theodore J.; Gambrill, Eileen D.; and Wiltse, Kermit T. Children in Foster Homes— Achieving Continuity of Care. New York: Praeger Publishers, 1978.

Walker, Florence C. "Cultural and Ethnic Issues in Working with Black Families in the Child Welfare System," in Parents of Children in Placement: Perspectives and Programs, edited by Paula A. Sinanoglu and Anthony N. Maluccio. New York: Child Welfare League of America, 1981, 133–148.

GROUP CHILD CARE CONSULTANT SERVICES

School of Social Work - University of North Carolina

300 Battle Hall 056-A Chapel Hill, North Carolina 27514

A RESOURCE FOR RESIDENTIAL GROUP CHILD CARE

Specializing in:
- CONSULTATION
- STUDIES
- TRAINING
- RESEARCH

Conducting:
- The Chapel Hill Workshops (July)
- Certificate Training Program (June)
- Winter Seminar (February)

*Contact us for information concerning:

The Basic Course For Residential Child Care Workers
A comprehensive course of study for adults who work with children in residential facilities. In seven modules covering topics such as THE GROUP, DISCIPLINE, SEPARATION, and DEVELOPMENTAL PLANNING.

Agency and Individual Memberships Invited

FOLIO

The manuscripts abstracted in this section were submitted to CHILD WELFARE. Length, or overlap with other articles, or limitation to specialized interests or particular geographical areas, prohibited publication in full. Readers may obtain a copy of the complete paper by writing to the author at the address given, including costs if noted. Requests for permission to reproduce papers should also be addressed to the author.

Title: **Families with Handicapped Children: Critical Events, Continuing Stress, and Professional Responses (19 pp.)**
Author: Robert Halpern, Ph.D.
Address: High/Scope Educational Research Foundation, 600 N. River Street, Ypsilanti, MI 48197
Cost: $2.50

This paper offers the clinical experience of a federally supported demonstration program (Direction Service) to assist handicapped children and their families through giving support and obtaining appropriate services. The 156 "children" ranged in age from birth to 25 years and spanned all types and degrees of mental and physical impairment. The author first describes the effects upon the family of having and trying to rear a handicapped child and the highly varied experiences of the family in dealing with professionals of different disciplines. He then discusses the many subjective difficulties professionals have in facing and intuiting the feelings and thoughts of these parents, thus inhibiting the quality of the support the parents so desperately need from them. Professionals working with these families have much to learn: "To support [the] parents in their roles without usurping parental rights and obligations is the most difficult task..."

Title: **Early Intervention and the Multidisciplinary Approach (17 pp.)**
Author: Grace C. Young, A.B.E.P.P.
Address: Greater Lawrence Early Intervention Program, 25 Central St., Andover, MA 01810
Cost: $3

Massachusetts law facilitates provision of special education for those aged 3 to 21 who cannot use regular classes. Early intervention programs, usually home-based, begin assessment and remedial work with developmentally disabled children before the age of 3, laying a groundwork with the children and their families for future special education. Helping the family is, of course, at least as important as helping the child. The psychologist-author of this paper describes, from her perspective, one such program that includes a professional nursery for the handicapped. The team comprises specialists from eight disciplines: physical therapy, speech pathology, occupational therapy, nutrition, psychology, social work, nursing, and teaching. How the specialists work together with child and family in a program of observation, evaluation, and treatment is presented in detail, with case illustrations.

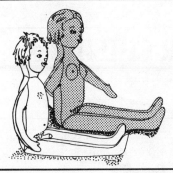
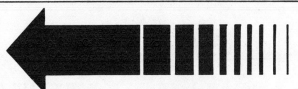

READERS' FORUM

Dear Editor:

"Permanency Planning: A Redefinition," by Anthony N. Maluccio and Edith Fein (CHILD WELFARE, May/June 1983), provides a very useful summary of the "state of the art" in achieving the optimal plan for children in foster care. The questions they raise about the possible implications of permanency planning are provocative; moreover, the brevity and straightforward writing of their article should make it possible for busy practitioners to quickly grasp their thoughtful discussion of such an important issue.

My one reservation about the article is that the authors do not distinguish between permanence as a legal status and a child's feeling of permanence. This distinction is suggested in two of Fanshel's studies and was clearly demonstrated in Lahti's follow-up study of the Oregon Project.

In their longitudinal study, Fanshel and Shinn developed an eight-item Index of Embedment in the Foster Care Setting. Findings indicated that children were rated by the caseworkers as substantially identified with their foster care setting after 3 years in care. Moreover, youngsters who entered care at a very young age were more likely to feel attached to their foster care setting than youngsters who entered when they were older.[1] Although a child's embedment in his or her foster care setting is not synonymous with the feeling of security assumed to be provided in a legally permanent setting, these findings do suggest that a child can feel some relatedness to an impermanent setting.

More recently, Fanshel studied 386 New York City foster children who had been in care for at least 1 year. Findings indicated that three-quarters of these youngsters were rated by their caseworkers as either being "deeply integrated" or "quite strongly identified" with their foster parents.[2] Here, again, there is a basis for differentiating between a child's status and his or her feelings about living arrangements.

As part of a larger follow-up study comparing youngsters who had received intensive services directed toward permanency planning and youngsters who had received "regular" child welfare services, Lahti interviewed 160 families

---

[1] Fanshel, David, and Shinn, Eugene B. Children in Foster Care. New York: Columbia University Press, 1978, 399–402.

[2] Fanshel, David. "Foster Children and Their Foster Parents," in On The Road to Permanency. New York: Child Welfare League of America, 1983, 255.

to assess their well-being. These 160 cases included youngsters (the numbers were not specified) who were reunited with their parents, adopted by new parents, adopted by foster parents, and still in foster care. Findings indicated that youngsters scoring highest on well-being were more likely to have a sense of permanence, as indicated by the caretaker's ability to plan for the future and to help the child with career planning, the child's involvement in family activities, and the interviewer's rating of the likelihood of the child's remaining in the foster home until age 18.

Lahti's permanency measure accounted for 30% of the variation in the children's well-being scores; in contrast, the type of placement accounted for only 7% of the variability in well-being scores. In commenting on these findings, Lahti concluded, "A sense of permanence was not necessarily related to the legal permanence of the placement. Perception of permanence occurred even without legal sanction, and it was absent even when legal sanctions were there."[3]

In citing these findings from Fanshel and Lahti, I do not mean to take issue with the policy of finding permanent homes for children. From my own work with foster children, I recall many who yearned to be reunited with their families and others who were happy to have an adoptive home. And, as we all know, many studies have documented the plight of foster children without family ties. Moreover, the program for permanency planning described by Maluccio and Fein is, in my view, a description of good social work practice and should be endorsed by whatever name.

In discussing permanency, however, I think it is important to make this distinction between permanence as a legal status and as a child's feelings of permanence. In most instances, it seems reasonable to assume that legal status and feelings of permanence will coincide; but I think this distinction is particularly helpful in making plans for the problematic cases where neither return to the home or adoption is a viable option.

Louise Murray, D.S.W.
Adjunct Assistant Professor
Fordham University
Graduate School of Social Service

[3] Lahti, Janet. "A Follow-Up Study of Foster Children in Permanent Placements." Social Service Review 56 (December 1982): 567–568.

Author's Reply

Edith Fein and I certainly appreciate Murray's thoughtful response to our article. Her point about the distinction between permanence as a legal status and as a child's sense of permanence is well taken. She is calling attention to a very important issue that we did not consider in our article. We have also been interested in Fanshel's and Lahti's findings on the child's sense of permanence and agree that it could have strong implications for policy and practice. These findings, however, are in general based on the reports of others, such as foster parents and caseworkers. Since it is even more crucial to explore the issue of the sense of permanence from the perspective of the child himself or herself, we carried out a small pilot study last year in which we attempted to learn how children placed in various permanent planning options perceived their "permanency status" in particular families. Although we did not come up with anything conclusive, and there were complex methodological and ethical issues involved in carrying out such a study by directly interviewing the child, we did feel that the issue of the child's sense of permanence should be further explored.

Anthony N. Maluccio, D.S.W.
Professor
University of Connecticut
School of Social Service

JOIN THE PURSUIT OF EXCELLENCE
JOIN THE CHILD WELFARE LEAGUE

For 62 years the League has worked to improve services to children in North America. Its member agencies have held to high standards of excellence as they reached out to dependent and neglected children. Now you can join in that cause. We invite you to become part of a network of agencies and individuals committed to "Guarding Children's Rights, Serving Children's Needs."

ORGANIZATION MEMBERSHIP   FEE
(Open to indirect service organizations. Membership
provides access to the Library Services and all CWLA
publications.) $400

INDIVIDUAL MEMBERSHIP
(Open to everyone who supports the purpose and
program of the League.)
    Contributor $300
    (Receives same entitlements as organization)
    Sustaining $100
    (Receives access to CWLA Library Services plus a
    choice of A, B, or C listed below.)
    Advocate $ 25
    (Access to the League's Library Services plus a
    choice of D or E listed below.)

Mail to: CWLA, 67 Irving Place, New York, NY 10003.

_____ Yes, I want to join CWLA. My check in the amount of _____ is enclosed. As a benefit of membership I wish to receive:

_____A (*CWLA Perspectives* and the "Special Publications Subscription," which
        includes the journal CHILD WELFARE and all new books and monographs
        published by CWLA during the calendar year.)
_____B (Washington-based newsletter *Child Welfare Planning Notes*)
_____C (CWLA *Crittenton Reporter on School Age Parenting*)
_____D (CWLA *Perspectives*)
_____E (Subscription to CHILD WELFARE)

NAME _____
                (please print)

ADDRESS _____

_____
                                                            (zip)

SIGNATURE _____ DATE _____ PI

CLASSIFIED ADVERTISEMENTS

Director—Residential Care Facility. Children's Farm Home, Corvallis, Oregon, is seeking a Director to assume duties on July 1, 1984. The Farm Home is a residential facility with a beautiful campus and several satellite centers. Located in the Willamette Valley, the Farm Home provides care and custody for adolescents from throughout Oregon. Current composite staff of 75 serving 83 students. A master's degree in management and/or social work and 12 years of experience in social work administration, or the equivalent combination of education and experience is required. Excellent fringe benefits. Salary commensurate with qualifications. Send resume and salary history in confidence to: Search Committee, P.O. Box 700, Corvallis, OR 97339, by December 1, 1983. EOE.

ADMINISTRATOR. A large multi-service organization is seeking a person with proven clinical and managerial skills to direct the programs of its children's service center and to provide clinical direction to the program directors. The center consists of a residential treatment program, emergency shelter, and a day treatment program. The person selected will work with a multi-disciplinary staff of 150+ employees. Responsibilities include organizational planning and evaluation, employee relations, budget management, and community relations.

Location in a residential neighborhood of a metro. area; urban and suburban benefits are readily available. Minnesota lakes and recreational opportunities at your doorstep.

Requirements: Ph.D. in clinical psychology with 5 years post-grad. experience or M.S.W. with 5 years of post-grad. experience, 3 of which are in administration. Residential or hospital experience desirable. Salary negotiable; liberal benefits. Please send resume to: Personnel, St. Joseph's Home for Children, 1121 East 46th Street, Minneapolis, MN 55407. EOE.

Executive Director of United Methodist children's home, Greeneville, Tennessee. Manage multi-purpose agency (residential, group homes, foster homes, adoption; 200 children; $1.7 million budget). Ten years' experience required. Principally, business management background required; also human services. Must be active Christian church member. Good benefits; salary negotiable. Send inquiries to P.O. Box 188, Greeneville, TN 37743.

Index to CHILD WELFARE
Volume LXII, 1983

This index is arranged by Subjects, Authors, and Book Reviews. The months are abbreviated as follows: January/February, J/F; March/April, M/A; May/June, M/J; July/August, J/A; September/October, S/O; November/December, N/D.

SUBJECTS

BOOK REVIEWS